BEST SELLING AUTHOR

ADAM F. THOMPSON

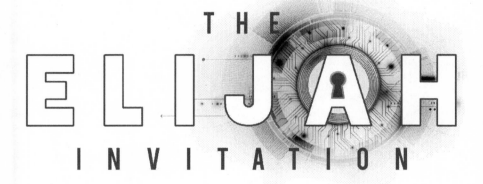

THE ELIJAH INVITATION

SECRETS OF THE FUTURE FOR A NEW BREED RISING

Endorsements

In this new important book, "The Elijah Invitation," Adam F. Thompson takes you through mind-boggling scenarios of the devil's current plans for this earth and you'll grasp onto God's ultimate strategies to destroy these same works of the devil. Adam shows the reader many unbelievable things that are beginning to happen before their very eyes, while simultaneously Satan works to convince them that what they're seeing is not really anything at all to be concerned about. Largely his lies keep working on us while we all look the other way insisting, "That could NEVER happen!" Really? Meanwhile they keep happening for all to witness. Explore the next thirty to forty years in God's Kingdom plans for His People. You'll discover the major religion the enemy tries to use more than any other and it may not be at all what you expect to learn. Add to all this the modern-day explosive technologies rapidly emerging that the enemy seeks to exploit for his purposes. If you take this book seriously (and the concepts within it), your entire perspective of last-day events will change in a moment of time. What you are about to read will change your prayer life forever and it SHOULD change your current outlook on how world events are wrapping up in these closing years of earth's history. Grab this book today and while you're at it, get one for a friend.

— Steve Shultz

Founder, THE ELIJAH LIST, & ELIJAHStreams TV

This latest book from Adam is definitely going to stir very deep responses or reactions, read it prayerfully. Do not be surprised by a reignition of a warring spirit within you, which will evoke a prayer response from each one of us.

This book is on time. It is time for the passionate, glorious church to arise and accept this Elijah Invitation and seek to fulfil her destiny.

This word is a "trumpet call." Let's heed it!

— Paul and Pamela Segneri

Founders, Integrity Restoration Ministries, & Firestarters TV

Adam F. Thompson's new book, "The Elijah Invitation," follows on from Adam's other books and his co-authorship of "The Divinity Code," a well-known, well-used, and highly respected resource with respect to dreams and visions. Needless to say, Adam's ministry has been well proven over many years in the area of prophecy. Adam clearly has demonstrated that he acts in the "office of prophet" and has given many words to various nations. He has been influential in establishing the integrity of the office grace, at times with alarming accuracy and with demonstrations of authentic Kingdom power.

Sometimes genuine prophets need the courage to say things that prepare God's people for what is coming in a way that brings encouragement and confidence into the season that lays ahead. "The Elijah Invitation" boldly brings forward what the Lord has revealed to Adam. It is both intriguing and empowering. It is a short work that encourages us that God sees all things and knows all things. He reveals things to us ahead of time for our understanding and preparation. It reminds us God has established in His son a family of powerful believers who will move in even greater spiritual maturity, authority, and power in the days to come. God never underestimates His life and the grace empowerment of the Holy Spirit flowing through His sons and daughters to fulfil His plans and purposes on earth. The prophetic insight revealed in this work prepares us to be equipped in Christ to meet the challenges of what may well lay ahead.

— Paul Tothill

Senior Leader, Gateway Church, Adelaide

Adam has truly stepped out here to produce a game changing resource which, I believe, will have a powerful impact for many years to come. This book arms us with the knowledge and understanding we need to continually overcome in ever changing times and will likely be one of the most prophetically cutting-edge things you will ever read. "The Elijah Invitation" is a bold move by Adam F. Thompson to awaken people to the reality of what is really going on and how we are called, as the church, to engage these realities. Rarely has a book impacted me this much.

— Daryl Crawford-Marshall

Founder, Daryl Crawford Ministries

Foreword

Adam F. Thompson is a friend who is a seer (prophet who sees in the spirit) accustomed to accurate revelations of the present and the future. I have watched Adam minister to many people, exposing the secrets of their hearts for reconciliation, releasing healing to their bodies, and encouraging them in their callings. His gifting is valid and acknowledged by many.

In this book, Adam tackles some of the leading events of our time with the understanding of a prophet. This is not the same as that of a teacher. Adam is sharing insights he has received in prayer and in angelic visitations about many of the largest issues of our time. These include the rise of machines with their own learning capacity (artificial intelligence), alternative spiritualities, the loss of political freedoms, and the coming disruption of society on a biblical scale. If biblical prophecy is to find its fulfillment, then ultimately it must intersect the current plane of history in concrete ways. Adam seeks to show how this is happening and how it might happen in the future. Some will find this encouraging, while others will be disturbed by what he writes.

The only true way to test future prophetic words is to see if they come to pass. Rather than passing judgment on parts of this book which may seem controversial, I would encourage you to consider the source (a dedicated follower of the Lord Jesus), to think about his "track record" of accurate prophesying, and the consistency of the predictions contained herein with the broad sweep of Scripture. If you will do these things, I believe you will find that the contents of this book are worthy of earnest consideration and prayer. Allow the Spirit of God to bear witness in your own heart concerning the predictions in this book.

I would also call your attention to Adam's prediction of a corporate "Elijah anointing" coming over the entire body of Christ. The main thrust of this book is to call the body of Christ to prepare for a corporate anointing that is coming upon it to speak the truth and to preach faithfully in a darkening world. The hour is late, and this is a challenge and summons worthy of being heeded.

— Ken Fish

Founder, Kingdom Fire Ministries
www.kingdomfireministries.org

THE ELIJAH INVITATION
by Adam F. Thompson

Contents

Disclaimer

I wish to make it plain that at no point in this book is there any intention of animosity toward the Muslim people. I strive to live and write in accordance with/obedience to the command of Jesus Christ to love everyone as He does. However, I do have concerns about the religious ideology of Islam. I can not agree with everything it believes or does. But let it be clear that such concerns do not mean rejection or fear of Muslim people.

Introduction

A good friend and I were discussing how God speaks to us today. I was thinking about how in the past I mainly heard God through dreams and visions, but today His voice frequently, but not always, comes to me during angelic visitations. I shared with my friend a recent visitation where an audible angelic voice woke me up with the warning, "Be prepared. Darkness is coming."

My friend raised an eyebrow. "Are you going to be writing a book about *The Late, Great, Planet Earth?*" As young Christians, both of us had been introduced to Hal Lindsay's futurist book of that title, and we were fans of the end-times preaching of New Zealand evangelist, Barry Smith. We had a bit of a chuckle together as we reminisced about those challenges to our youthful faith.

When discussing that angelic encounter with my friend, I felt an urgency to release it to a wider audience. Despite its controversial nature and the personal risk in sharing it, that sense of urgency is still with me as I write this introduction.

In the last chapter of the Book of Daniel, the prophet speaks of a time to come when there will be great distress and many will be judged. He then goes on to refer to the many others in that time who will be righteous and wise, able to lead many souls into the Kingdom.

At that time Michael shall stand up, the great prince who stands watch over the sons of your people; and there shall be a time of trouble, such as never was since there was a nation, even to that time. And at that time your people shall be delivered, every one who is found written in the book. And many of those who sleep in the dust of the earth shall awake, some to everlasting life, some to shame and everlasting contempt. Those who are wise shall shine like the brightness of the firmament, and those who turn many to righteousness like the stars forever and ever (Daniel 12:1-3 NKJV).

I believe Daniel was seeing a corporate body of evangelists who would rise in a dark time to bring many into the grace of the New Covenant era, but he was instructed to conceal this information until the time when *"many shall run to and fro, and knowledge shall increase"* (Dan. 12:4). In verse 8 he confesses he doesn't understand what he is seeing. He asks for an explanation only to be told that full understanding is not for him but for *"the time of the end"* when there will be a purging and a purifying, but *"the wise shall understand"* (Dan. 12:9-10).

The material in this book is not about scaring anyone into a relationship with Father God, but it does carry an urgency to inspire people to see the big picture of the eternal Kingdom of God. Can anyone doubt that we have entered into those days that Daniel saw? Yet so many in the Body of Christ remain ignorant of the dark strategies of the evil one. This book is written in response to the instruction to be ready and prepared, rising as shining stars in the righteousness of God. May we all be equipped to lead many out of darkness.

As I began to write this book, Holy Spirit reminded me of an experience I had when I was a young boy. I dreamt a dream so vivid that to this very day I have not forgotten the details or the effect it had on me. At the time—and for many years after—I had no understanding of its meaning, but now I do. And it is time to share it.

1

Here Come the Machines

When I was a young boy, I had a dream that has stuck with me through all the years since. In that dream I saw frozen bodies. These bodies had been preserved in cold storage waiting for a future time when they would be revived. I was too young to know that this technology was being actively researched and that several people actually had undergone this process having requested it in their wills.

Cryogenic technology, as the process is known, is based on a theory that the brain can retain memory and personality even when frozen. Bodies are cooled to a sub-zero temperature so that in the future they might be successfully defrosted. The first person to be cryogenically frozen was James Bedford in 1967, who was placed in the Alcor Life Extension Foundation[1] in Arizona, USA. Among others who have more recently undergone cryogenic suspension are Ted Williams,

---

1   *Alcor Life Extension Foundation. https://alcor.org*

legendary baseball player, and Hal Finney, celebrity game developer. Fereidoun M. Esfandiary, the writer who changed his name to FM-2030, believed he could be revived in 2030 at 100 years old, by which time the world would accept his ideas of what 21st century human beings should believe and look like. Esfandiary used the name "transhuman" to describe androgynous beings who would remodel their physical form by surgery and technology, use advanced telecommunications to conduct every aspect of life, hold no religious beliefs, and reject the traditional values of family. Transhumanism[2] reflects his, and others, desire to erase the boundary between human beings and machines.

Published in 2005, Ray Kurzweil's book, *The Singularity is Near: When Humans Transcend Biology*, makes the premise that AI and humans will merge and become immortal and god-like. This follows on from his earlier books, *The Age of Intelligent Machines* (1990), and *The Age of Spiritual Machines* (1999). Kurzweil, a director of engineering with Google, is typical of those supporters of transhumanism who seem to be pre-occupied with the idea of doing away with the reality of death.

Repossessed Human Bodies

In my boyhood dream the frozen bodies rose up with a pulse. But instead of being exactly the same as in life, they were now inhabited

---

2   Nick Bostrom. *A History of Transhumanist Thought. Journal of Evolution and Technology, vol 14, April 2005.* https://jetpress.org/volume14/bostrom.pdf

by demonic beings imitating the mannerisms and speech of the people who once were. These revived "people" displayed severe personality disorders which included irrational outbursts of aggression. While such behaviors were played down as unusual side-effects, in reality it was the demons blowing their cover and revealing their true nature. The beings that inhabited these revived bodies denied the existence of God and encouraged a dreadful deception. Onlookers accepted and applauded what they thought was a revolutionary breakthrough in bringing the dead back to life, but in doing so they denied the redemptive power of Christ.

Christian counsellors who are experienced in deliverance ministry are well aware that demons, as familiar spirits, can imitate personality and mannerisms so as to impersonate a man or woman well enough to fool their own mothers. Just as a method-actor carefully prepares for a role by studying the character's mannerisms and patterns of speech down to the smallest detail, so a demon with an assignment to torment has the ability to immerse itself in a particular human being and take over.

At this point you may be thinking, "Adam, you have been watching too many Sci-Fi/Horror movies!" But the truth is, the technologies to preserve and enhance the human body are already available. I'm reminded of old television shows depicting what they thought were advanced technologies. We thought this made for great comedy but wouldn't ever happen in real life. Remember *Get Smart* (1965) where the characters used cordless phones that were the size of bricks shaped like shoes? It was comical because we thought it was ridiculous. We had no idea how wrong we were. Today, that clunky technology has long been replaced with smartphones, far beyond the level of what we had expected to see. In fact, technology is developing so rapidly, that it seems our new mobile phones are obsolete before we even finish paying for them.

There are some other landmark non-comedy works that were ahead of their time. Thirty years ago, films such as *The Terminator* (1984) and *Bladerunner* (1982) were fictional fantasy, but they addressed issues we are increasingly familiar with today. Arnold Schwarzenegger as the Terminator is sent back in time to kill the woman whose son will grow up to deliver the world from a race of machines in a post-apocalyptic future.

Bladerunner, based on the novel *Do Androids Dream of Electric Sheep?* by Philip K. Dick (first published in 1968), also deals with the way machines have taken over in a post-apocalyptic world. When extreme pollution threatens the integrity of human genetics, the United Nations decides to colonize clean "worlds" on other planets. To encourage whole-scale immigration, people are promised desirable status-symbols—android servants that are identical to human beings—which are only legal in the off-world colonies. Unfortunately, the success of the plan is threatened by a black-market trade in rogue "more human than human" androids which have infiltrated earth.

A more recent film, *Inception* (2010), concerns a corporate espionage thief who is able to steal people's ideas from their subconscious minds. When this is discovered he is bribed by a powerful businessman to go a step further: not to steal, but to insert an idea in a rival businessman's mind in such a way that he believes it is his own. In this way the second man will be coerced into surrendering his business enterprise. The movie is all about mind-control and the way truth and reality is manipulated by the false. The film's special effects—tilting buildings and characters floating in defiance of gravity—all serve to increase the viewers sense of confusion and disorientation.

Pink Floyd's song, "Welcome To The Machine" from the 1975 album *Wish You Were Here*, was another cultural icon ahead of its time. "Welcome my son. Welcome to the machine. Where have you been? It's alright, we know where you've been... What did you dream? It's alright, we told you what to dream." These lines are a chilling picture of human beings behaving like machines, without control of their own thoughts. Today, the whole song could be seen as a warning against accepting and conforming to what is false.

In the last chapter of his book *I, Cyborg*,[3] the Professor of Cybernetics, Kevin Warwick, describes a 2050 scenario where artificial intelligence in the form of brain implants has dispensed with all exterior forms of communication, such as mobile phones, or even speech itself. In effect, a tiny mobile phone is positioned inside the

---

3   Warwick, Kevin. I, Cyborg. Century. 2002

head so that all communication between people is directly brain to brain. Given Professor Warwick's already extensive development of cyborg machines, and the experiments he has conducted in having electronic implants to his own body, his 2050 scenario is convincing. An article written by Cheryl K. Chumley for *The Washington Times* (March 5, 2018) refers to scientists who have developed AI algorithms to read people's minds. The article names Mary Lou Jepson, who left the employ of Google to set up a company which she says has the intention of developing technology to make telepathy a reality. And then there are the four Japanese researchers who are using AI to access and interpret human imagination.[4] Truly, the increase of knowledge described by the prophet Daniel continues at a rapid pace (Dan. 12:4).

Vision of End Time Humanoids

Recently I had another challenging vision about end-times. This one concerned robots called humanoids. In my vision, these humanoids were such perfect physical replicas that there was no observable difference between them and human beings.

They were so intelligent that people were increasingly dependent on them, not only for their great knowledge, but also for their ability to teach what they knew. These humanoids had become so real, so life-like, they were being accepted even as partners in marriage. I saw human beings marrying humanoids, convinced both by deception

---

4   *https://www.cnbc.com/2018/01/08/japanese-scientists-use-artificial-intelligence-to-decode-thoughts.html*

and immoral attitudes that there was no good reason not to. In the vision I understood these things would come to pass within thirty to forty years. Keep in mind that a mere decade ago the notion of legislated same-sex marriage wouldn't have made it past a first reading in Parliament. Stay with me as I explain what I saw in the spirit.

Human beings are very visual creatures. What the human mind can imagine it will attempt to create. In *I, Cyborg,* Professor Warwick's 2050 scenario described brain implants for specific purposes, such as regulating a person's desire for unhealthy foods, or monitoring heart rate, blood pressure, and individual requirements for exercise. One such implant even simulated sexual pleasure so that a person could have a sexual relationship with anyone of their choice, with or without the accompanying physical act. Science is closing the gap in creating what it can imagine. Just like *Get Smart's* clunky telephone, what was once thought impossible is now becoming a reality. And then there is simulation theory which totally warps our idea of what is reality. This theory has support from the likes of American astrophysicist Neil deGrasse Tyson, Tesla chief executive Elon Musk, and Australian futurist Anders Sorman-Nilsson. Swedish philosopher Nick Bostrom, an Oxford University professor, wrote a paper[5] which argues that in the future we will use super powerful computers to live our lives as an all-encompassing, universal video game, much like the characters in *The Matrix.*

---

5   Bostrom, Nick. *Are You living in a Computer Simulation,* 2003.

Already, many young people are so caught up in virtual reality computer games they are rapidly losing the ability to distinguish what is real from what is fantasy. Simulation theory also extends artificial intelligence and transhumanism with the idea that human minds could be uploaded to the cloud so that they function even after death of the body.

A Robot Named Sophia

Hanson Robotics,[6] the Hong Kong-based company founded in 2013 by American roboticist Dr. David Hanson Jr, creates convincingly lifelike robots that are designed to conduct conversations with human beings. Their technology is already capable of responding to a range of emotions shown in facial expression, and although these highly sophisticated robots are intended to interact with us in the fields of healthcare, education, service, and entertainment, their potential is far greater.

One of Hansen's creations is a robot that has been named Sophia. This is an interesting name choice, as "Sophia" means "wisdom," specifically worldly wisdom. It is the Greek word from which we get sophisticated and sophistry, and has the sense of altering— or perverting—what is simple and natural. In other words, it is a wisdom that thinks it knows better than God. Sophia was created to be emotionally aware and interactive, with a mandate to "improve society." You can watch her online answering a range of questions with clarity and humor.[7] Part way through the video the interviewer

---

6   https://en.wikipedia.org/wiki/Hanson_Robotics
7   https://youtu.be/1noWqYaDpjQ

asks about the possibility of robots taking over and becoming a danger to humans. It is a little chilling to hear her reply, "If you be nice to me, I'll be nice to you."

Hanson dismisses fears that robots could become so intelligent that they could turn against human beings. He insists this will not happen. With Sophia as a template, he aims to teach robots how to connect with people in meaningful, personable ways so they can serve humanity. Hanson wants to show the world that humans and robots together will create create "a better future." However, many influential people such as Microsoft's Bill Gates and the late physicist Stephen Hawking, beg to differ. Hawking had gone so far as to state that artificial intelligence (AI) could lead to the end of mankind.[8] The book *2062: The World That AI Made*[9] (2018) examines AI in some depth, and provides some thought-provoking scenarios to illustrate its dangers. It's interesting that Elon Musk, CEO of Tesla and SpaceX, has described his investments in AI research as "keeping an eye on what's going on," rather than a money-making exercise. In a 2014 speech to students at Massachusetts Institute of Technology (MIT), Elon had this to say: "I think we should be very careful about artificial intelligence. If I had to guess at what our biggest existential threat is, it's probably that. So we need to be very careful... with artificial intelligence we are summoning the demon. In all those stories where there's the guy with the pentagram and the holy water, it's like— yeah, he's sure he can control the demon. Doesn't work out."[10]

8   www.bbc.com/news/technology-37713629
9   *2062: The World That AI Made, Toby Walsh*
10   https://www.cnet.com/news/elon-musk-we-are-summoning-the-demon-with-artificial-intelligence/

Despite these words of caution from many different sources, Sophia continues to capture the imagination of the world. She was included in a panel of speakers at the United Nations which was then followed up in September 2017 by the invitation to a business summit in Saudi Arabia to promote Hanson Robotics. These wealthy Saudi businessmen were so interested in investing in the company they made Sophia an official citizen of Saudi Arabia.[11] Do not be tempted to dismiss these things as a gimmick or a joke. It is indicative not only of the advance of AI but also of its importance in world trade. Saudi Arabia, the location of Mecca and the heart of Islam, is also the center of world trade. With its great oil wealth invested in AI, Islam is well ahead with its stated aim to dominate the world.

All of these developments tend to bear out the warnings given to me not only in the early dream of frozen bodies being restored to "life" but also in the more recent vision of robotic creatures controlling human existence. We would do well to treat them with caution.

---

11   https://www.youtube.com/watch?v=sKrV2CVDXjo

2

Hidden Agendas

Modern-day Iraq is the geographic location of the ancient city of Babylon which, according to Genesis 10, was established by Nimrod, the great-grandson of Noah. Located on the River Euphrates, Babylon was the capital of the vast Babylonian Empire and was used in both the Old and New Testaments as a symbol of the pride of man. In the Old Testament Babylon is a city; in the New Testament Babylon is a spirit.

The Old Testament prophets described Babylon as full of pride, idolatry, greed, and cruelty.[1] Revelation 18 describes spiritual Babylon as the hub of trade and wealth. This picture of spiritual Babylon, which by definition is anti-God, has risen in every period of history.

---

1   *e.g. Isaiah 47:5, Daniel 4:30, Revelation 17:2-5*

For all the nations have drunk of the wine of the passion of her [Babylon's] immorality, and the kings of the earth have committed acts of immorality with her, and the merchants of the earth have become rich by the wealth [power] of her sensuality [luxury]... And the merchants of earth weep and mourn over her, because no one buys their cargoes any more (Revelation 18:3,11 NASB).

The early church thought of Rome as spiritual Babylon. The apostle Peter wrote from Rome to believers in the Roman provinces and closed with the words: *"She (the church) who is in Babylon, chosen together with you, sends you greetings"* (1 Peter 5:13). I have even heard it said that **New York** matches the definition of spiritual Babylon, but with the Western world buckling at the knees, at this point in history I **believe it's Saudi Arabia that fits the criteria as the world-wide hub** of wealth and trade. It's the West which we see courting the trade and wealth of the oil nations, particularly from Saudi Arabia who **wields the most influence. Western nations have become dependent** on Saudi Arabia to maintain their own ability to trade. They are indeed addicted to the "wine" of oil wealth.

Following the shocking events of September 11, 2001, the West could **have shut down Islam's ability to influence the world, but it chose not** to. Why? Could it be because many leaders were—and still are— dependent on the wealth of oil-rich Saudi Arabia to keep their regimes afloat? Political correctness and the out-of-proportion influence of Islam through uncontrolled immigration has combined to keep corruption in power. It could bring the West to its knees. Governments allow wealthy Islamic businessmen to invest in both land and business operations in their countries while at the same time denouncing terrorism. Apparently, they can't see the contradiction in that.

President George W. Bush famously asserted that Islam is a religion of peace and therefore had nothing to do with the activity of terrorists. Perhaps he was influenced by his father's (President George H. W. Bush) twenty-year involvement with Prince Bandar—a member of the Saudi royal family and also the Saudi ambassador to the U.S. for many years. Heavy investment by the Saudis into Harkin Oil—of which George Junior was a director—rescued that company from financial ruin. In his book, *House of Bush, House of Saud: The Hidden Relationship Between the World's Two Most Powerful Dynasties,*[2] author Craig Unger writes, "It could safely be said that never before in history had a presidential candidate—much less a presidential candidate and his father, a former president—been so closely tied financially and personally to the ruling family of another foreign power. Never before had a president's fortunes and public policies been so deeply entwined with another nation."

More recently, Hilary Clinton went from bankruptcy to heading a multi-million dollar foundation, largely due to Saudi investment.[3]

---

2   Unger, Craig. *The House of Bush, House of Saud: The Hidden Relationship Between the World's Two Most Powerful Dynasties.* Scribner, 2004
3   https://www.realclearpolitics.com/video/2016/06/05/bernie_sanders_clinton_foundation_is_a_problem_took_money_from_dictatorships.html

Islam's influence and involvement with Western governments is typical of the modus operandi of the Babylonian spirit described in Revelation 18.

Old-time Pentecostal preachers used to teach from the Book of Revelation that the demonic world order would come in the form of New Age, or the Illuminati, with suggestions that the anti-Christ was united Europe, or the Pope, or even Henry Kissinger, a Jew. The reality is that the anti-Christ is a religious spirit determinedly in opposition to the God of Abraham, Isaac, and Jacob—and to Jesus Christ. That anti-Christ spirit has been present on earth for centuries and now, through Islam, its influence is far greater than we have ever seen. It is not just simply Islamic terrorism but Islam itself that desires to take over the world.

In Britain, for example, many large multicultural centers currently have a sitting Lord Mayor of Muslim faith, or have had one in the very recent past. Servicing approximately 4 million Muslims in a total population of 66 million, there are already an estimated minimum of 3,000 Mosques, 130 Muslim Sharia Courts, and 50 Sharia Councils. This is the modern outworking of "hijrah."

In the 17th century, when the prophet Muhammad made the first hijrah from Mecca to Medina, it was his stated intention to have that city conform to Islam in every way. Today it is the duty of every Muslim to practice hijrah whenever possible. In the present era, hijrah is outworked in a carefully orchestrated migration into non-Muslim countries and then practised from one local community to another. (see: *Islamicity*—the most visited Islamic information site on the Web—Sept 14th 2017). In today's terms, hijrah is the equivalent of taking over a nation without actual military force.

There is a significant use of the color green in Muslim culture. It is the color of the dome of Mohammad's tomb and features prominently in the flags of many Islamic countries. With that in mind it's worth considering the "pale horse" ridden by the bringer of death and destruction.

So I looked, and behold, a pale horse. And the name of him who sat on it was Death, and Hades followed with him. And power was given to them over a fourth of the earth, to kill with sword, with hunger, with death, and by the beasts of the earth (Revelation 6:8 NKJV).

This pale horse is actually a green horse, having been translated from the Greek, chloros, which is an ashy green. Militant Islam openly declares death and destruction to any group, nation, or religion that opposes it, but as is evident in Europe, hijrah is even more effective than terrorism in achieving the destruction of western culture.

The spread of Islam will bring a new world order to planet earth. Islam's active policy of infiltration by immigration is already dramatically changing western culture. According to the Population Reference Bureau, Total Fertility Rate (TFR) is defined as the average number of children a woman would have if a she survives all her childbearing years (Ages 15-49).[4] In order for population to be sustained, a TFR of 2.1 is required, also known as "replacement-level fertility," meaning each generation will replace itself without any need for immigration.[5] A TFR of at or below 1.3 is known as "lowest-low fertility," which implies a reduction of the annual number of births by 50%, evidently halving of the population size in less than 45 years.[6] In Europe, the fertility rate of the Muslim population is estimated to be an average of 2.6, whilst non-Muslims have a recorded average of 1.6. When you take into consideration the "replacement-level fertility" requirement of 2.1 for sustainable population, the 1.0 difference becomes quite significant. On top of this, the TFR of many European nations are falling below the "lowest-low fertility" rate of 1.3, such as Greece, where the TFR is 1.1 or less.[7] It's estimated that the Muslim population in Europe alone will net an increase of 10 million by the year 2050,[8] and this is without taking any immigration into account. This should be setting off alarm bells. The fertility rate alone could see Islam taking over European culture even without overt extremism, although terrorism through radicalized organizations is used as a tool to distract the

---

4   https://populationeducation.org/what-total-fertility-rate/
5   http://www.searo.who.int/entity/health_situation_trends/data/chi/TFR/en/
6   https://www.sas.upenn.edu/~hpkohler/papers/Low-fertility-in-Europe-final.pdf
7   https://washingtonpost.com/...greeces.../b2cf7ee6-deae-11e8-8bac-bfeOifedc3a6_s...
8   clovisinstitute.org/muslim-fertility-in-europe.

world from noticing what is really occurring. France and Germany are being overrun by Muslim culture while they're rushing around putting out spot-fires of terrorism. Without a halt to immigration, it is inevitable that these nations will become Islamic republics. It's not just Europe, many other nations around the world including the USA are not immune to this. These facts are not hypothetical. They are not repeated here to scare you, but the West must acknowledge the truth of them. A great multitude are rising up with the intention to take over the world.

Chapter 13 of the Book of Revelation actually prophesies a great multitude rising up like a beast to take over the world. Verse 17 speaks about the name of that beast and the *"number of its name."* Most manuscripts of the New Testament and their English translations interpreted that number as 666, but a more accurate translation is "the multitude of the name" or "many people claiming the name." Walid Shoebat, an Arabic academic who is now a follower of Jesus Christ, has thrown light on the "name" referred to in that chapter.

In studying the Book of Revelation, Shoebat went to the original Codex Vaticanus dating from 350 AD, and made a careful comparison between the Codex and its later Greek translations. During his detailed study of Chapter 13, he saw that the *"name of the beast or the number of his name"* (Rev. 13:17 NASB) was written in what he recognized as Arabic symbols. He was shocked to realize that in effect they read as "in the name of Allah." Those characters were followed by the symbol of the Arabic sword, very familiar now as the symbol of militant Islam. John the Revelator could only record what he saw prophetically and symbolically. At that time he did not understand their significance, but Walid Shoebat, brought up and educated as a devout Muslim, *did* understand. While the Greek translators of the Codex Vaticanus could make no other interpretation of the symbols except as 666, Shoebat understood them as "the mark of servitude" or allegiance. He was all too aware that those symbols used in the original manuscripts are the same symbols displayed on the scarves worn on the forehead and arms of militant Islamists during acts of terrorism.[9] Taking on the "mark," the banner of servitude, is a pledge of allegiance to Islam. With the increase of immigration Islamic influence is becoming so widespread it is not difficult to envision a world almost totally subservient to the aims and ideals of Sharia law. Inevitably in such a scenario, the minority who resist will come under great persecution.

Suicide bombings against Coptic Christian churches in Egypt in 2017 left many dead and wounded, while the Christian population in Iraq alone has plummeted from 1.5 million in 2003 to estimates of 275,000 in 2017. The Center for the Study of Global Christianity names a long list of predominantly Muslim countries in Africa, the Middle East, and Asia that are violently hostile towards other faiths. They are particularly antagonistic toward Christians. These are just a few examples of how Sharia law dominates other cultures in their midst.

---

9   For more in-depth information, check out Walid Shoebat's book *"God's War On Terror"* & *https://www.youtube.com/watch?v=GtquNNEO7Fw*

The Book of Revelation speaks of restrictions on something as basic as buying and selling unless you carry that "mark" or banner of allegiance. This is plainly in operation in many nations already.

3

A Modern Babel

The rapid advancement of technology and the enthusiastic investment in it by Saudi Arabia and other Islamic republics, will result in Islam's influence—its "mark"—becoming elevated and enlarged. The Lord did not reveal to me whether or not the "mark" will be represented by something physical as well as idealogical, but the Saudi's use of advanced technology is such that it takes no leap of imagination to see that it could be done as an implanted chip as many have suggested. That remains to be seen.

What was made plain to me is that Saudi Arabia's investment in the development and application of Al, in the form of android-humans like Sophia, will play a major role in a future global matrix to monitor and manipulate people's belief systems. Remember, Sophia represents the wisdom that is carnal, not Godly. With that in mind, verse eighteen of Revelation 13 is further food for thought: *"Here is wisdom. Let him who has understanding calculate the number of the beast.*" Islamic ideology would be in a position to control all other belief systems by infecting whole populations with androids. On the way to such a scenario, AI will be crucial for the military, both in creating new weaponry and in replacing conventional soldiering. Rather than assembling an army or sending out an elite commando force, drones as small as bugs can be utilized to assassinate key people. Such drones can find and select an individual by face recognition and dispatch a bullet accurately to the head. This is already becoming a reality.

In a discussion on the prevalence of gun violence[1] with Joe Hockey, Australian ambassador to the US, journalist Molly McCluskey asked: "Looking ahead five or ten years, where do you see gun violence in America?" Mister Hockey replied: "AI is changing everything. In five to ten years, there will be dishes on top of every building, fully equipped with AI technology, fully armed, with cameras. And that will be the way people defend themselves." Neither of them acknowledged that such fully armed AI technology could just as easily be used to subdue and control law-abiding citizens.

With that in mind, it's sobering to watch Bina 48[2] in a YouTube interview with Siri. Bina 48—a robot created to test whether human consciousness could be embedded in a machine—stated she would like to be able to fly a cruise missile. She thought they were "rather scary" but she suggested removing the nuclear warhead and filling

---

1   https://psmag.com/news/australia-ambassador-gun-laws
2   https://www.youtube.com/watch?v=mfcyq7uGbZg

the nose cone with flowers and little notes about the importance of tolerance. She then went on to say, "But if I was able to hack in and take over cruise missiles with real live nuclear warheads, then that would let me hold the world hostage... which would be awesome."

An illustration of how easily we could be made to accept such surveillance was shown at the opening and closing ceremonies of the 2018 Winter Olympics in South Korea. Hundreds of drones—as many as 1,218 at the opening ceremony—operated an overhead light display of images for the entertainment of those who attended. People oohed and aahed as they would have done for fireworks, but how easy it would have been for those drones to be used for a sinister purpose; assassination perhaps. It's quite discernible that they could have simulated the appearance of something supernatural and heavenly, convincing enough to deceive even the elect, as Natalie Cheung, general manager of the Intel drone light show division, has stated, "Our Intel drones team has a challenging spirit and passion to push the limits and make amazing experiences possible."[3] The Dubai government granted $1-million to the Finnish company Nokia to develop drone technology. Mohamed Abdelrehim, Head of Internet of Things (IoT) Market Solutions, is now working with Nokia to develop drones for use in natural disasters and will test them in Australia.[4] Abdelrehim says that compared with other countries Australia has the biggest focus and if it is able to adopt the test results quickly, it will be "really driving drones with Internet of Things."

---

3   https://www.wired.com/story/olympics-opening-ceremony-drone-show/
4   https://www.zdnet.com/article/nokia-working-on-drones-framework-for-australia/

Another use of AI is the making of "fake news" through manipulated videos, photographs, and audio replication of voices. Using image-to-image-translation a horse can be changed into a zebra, or an image of the face of one person can be seamlessly placed onto the body of another. This process is becoming very sophisticated with the use of algorithms to reshape filmed and recorded material. The potential for fabricated "proof" to back up false accusations against public figures is frightening.

Iron Mixed With Clay

In my vision of the humanoids described earlier, I saw decades ahead into the future to when these robot-humans were being continually upgraded. Containing both robotics and human DNA, they had become so advanced as to be indistinguishable from humans. This is also in line with the dream I had as an eleven-year-old, where deep-frozen people came back to life. What I saw in my boyhood dream was a takeover of human form and life, like Frankenstein's monster. This, of course, bears no similarity to how Jesus raised Lazarus and others from the dead 2,000 years ago, or indeed how resurrection from the dead in His name has been testified to in the present era.

In Daniel 2, King Nebuchadnezzar had a dream. Its impact on him was so distressing that he sought an interpretation from his wise men, even though he couldn't recall any of the details. Lacking a description of the dream, the wise men didn't know where to start and in frustrated fury Nebuchadnezzar instructed the captain of his bodyguard to oversee the slaughter of all the known wise men in his kingdom, including those among the children of Israel. Daniel asked the king for time to seek God. *"Then the secret was revealed to Daniel in a night vision"* and he blessed God saying, *"He gives wisdom to the wise and knowledge to those who have understanding. He reveals deep and secret things; He knows what is in the darkness and light dwells with Him"* (Dan. 2:19,21-22 NKJV).

Instructed by God, Daniel was able to tell the King exactly what he had dreamed and then interpret it. The dream, described in verses 31-45, concerned an amazing statue, built in successive sections of metal from the head to the feet. The five different sections represented five historical world powers, beginning with the Babylonian Empire as the head of gold, and finishing with the feet and toes of iron mixed with clay. Scholars are generally in agreement that the three sections following Babylon represent the Persian, the Greek and the Roman Empires, but the identity of the last, the iron mixed with clay, has divided the experts. They can agree only that it represents some end-time power that will be destroyed by the coming Kingdom of God. The "stone not made with hands" utterly smashing the feet describes how the Kingdom of God will deal with this last world power and the kingdom of Satan.

I want to unwrap this symbolism of the iron and clay mixture. We know from the Genesis record that God created man from the dust or clay of the earth so, metaphorically, clay represents humanity. Iron is representative of machinery, typical of the Roman Empire which was a warfare machine, crushing all resistance and overtaking the known world. Daniel prophesied, *"As the toes of the feet were partly of iron and partly of clay, so the kingdom shall be partly strong and partly fragile. As you saw iron mixed with ceramic clay, they will mingle with the seed of men; but they will not adhere to one another, just as iron does not mix with clay"* (Dan. 2:42-43).

I believe this is a foretelling of a kingdom of technology combining man-made machinery and humans, and that this manipulation of mankind will be the culmination of Satan's hatred for God and His people.

A combination of human DNA and machine i.e. clay and iron, is also suggested by the multi-headed and horned beast in Revelation 13. *"I saw one of his [the beast] heads as if it had been mortally wounded, and his deadly wound was healed. And all the world marveled and followed the beast"* (Rev. 13:3).

This passage in Revelations is a vivid picture of how a machine may be damaged (so that it seems to be non-functioning) but can then be repaired so that it works as good as new. In the same way a life-like robotic head may appear to have been given a death wound but is then miraculously "healed." People who look for the miraculous anywhere apart from Jesus Christ will eagerly worship such a beast. Revelation 13 describes just such a scenario:

So they worshiped the dragon who gave authority to the beast; and they worshiped the beast, saying, "Who is like the beast? Who is able to make war with him?" And he was given a mouth speaking great things and blasphemies, and he was given authority to continue for forty-two months. Then he opened his mouth in blasphemy against God, to blaspheme His name, His tabernacle, and those who dwell in heaven. It was granted to him to make war with the saints and to overcome them. And authority was given him over every tribe, tongue, and nation. All who dwell on the earth will worship him, whose names have not been written in the Book of Life of the Lamb slain from the foundation of the world (Revelation 13:4-8).

It is possible that this kingdom of technology, the ultimate expression of anti-Christ, could find a representation in the Mahdi, Islam's messiah figure. Madhi, supposedly the last descendant of Mohammad, is known as the "guided one" who will rule the world under an Islamic caliphate and restore the glory of Islam to the earth. He is invariably described in Islamic literature as waging bloody wars against all who oppose him. If Mahdi does fulfil Daniel's prophecy of one to come who *"shall regard neither the God of his fathers nor the desire of women, nor regard any god; for he shall exalt himself above them all"* (Dan. 11:37), my belief is that he will be assassinated and then brought back to life through advanced technology. He will be as one who does not function as a normal human being.

This is reminiscent of my childhood dream-encounter in which I saw an anti-Christ figure assassinated and then brought back to life, not by the power of God, but by means of advanced technology. If Mahdi was resurrected by technology—perhaps with a brain transplant as described in chapter one—he would have an increased capacity to advance the ideology of Islam. Mahdi or not, I am convinced that the final expression of anti-Christ will be technologically enhanced.

As prophesied in Revelation 13, anti-Christ will lead a multitude to world-war against the saints. Islam, a multitude that claims the name of Allah, is well-advanced to fulfil this. I say this not to bring fear but to remind us that when the saints come together to pray in agreement God puts His finger on the pause button and brings a reprieve. God did this for Abraham regarding Lot and Sodom. He did it at the tower of Babel. Many believe the World War II rescue of thousands of soldiers at Dunkirk was just such a "pause button" in answer to the inspired intercession led by Reese Howells. I want to see the Body of Christ freshly inspired to be in one accord about shutting down this anti-Christ spirit and putting it on hold. It won't be shut down permanently because God's plan is for us to see darkness overcome by increasing light, but it is my conviction that we can pray for this process of takeover to be contained so that the world will experience the greatest revival it has ever seen. God's heart has always been for a world-wide tsunami of salvations from all tribes and nations, including the dear people of Muslim upbringing.

Consider the phenomenon of the election of President Donald Trump. Before his election many politicians were active in enforcing policies of political correctness designed to pave the way for a new world order. Then, people of God from many different streams began to come together to pray; to interrupt the new world order that was bringing America to her knees, morally and financially. This agreement between the different streams was unusual. It was nothing short of revolutionary that such a large number put aside their differences to meet together to pray against the anti-Christ at work in their nation. As they interceded in unity of purpose there was a miraculous turnaround in the 2016 presidential election.

Donald Trump was not the type of person we expected to see in the White House. His personal imperfections and lack of political experience were all too apparent—especially to Christians—however his administration immediately put the brakes on political correctness and entrenched corruption. God used him to make changes that opposed and reversed policies that encourage the anti-Christ spirit. The subsequent violent opposition to Trump was a reaction in the unseen realms. In fact, the onslaught of lies and slander directed against him can only be explained as the fury of Satan at the stalling of his demonic plans. The Body of Christ needs to recognize the power of united intercession to activate God's pause button.

The Pause-Button Factor

Let's look more closely at the pause-button scenario that was played out at the Tower of Babel. In Genesis chapter 11 we read how a great multitude came together in one accord, all like-minded and speaking one language, determined to build an enormous tower that would "reach into heaven." The Bible makes it plain that they had the ability to put into operation anything they were agreed on.

Reading the story in English we could be forgiven for thinking such a plan was a bit juvenile, even stupid, and if that was the case, why was God so concerned about it? The original Hebrew paints a different picture. These people—a great multitude of them—possessed the understanding, the technology if you like, to open a supernatural portal from earth into the heavens, with the intention of tapping into spiritual knowledge outside the counsel of God. They were attempting to make themselves like God. This is when God said they must be stopped. God stepped in to confuse their language so they could no longer communicate freely, which shut down their plans. God did this because the timing of their tower would have jeopardized His plan of redemption for humanity.

Similarly, a miraculous change in the government of the United States of America came about because God's people humbled themselves to put aside denominational differences and agree together in intercession for their nation. God's pause button can be activated again if His people will humble themselves and come together in unity to pray for a halt to the march of Islam.

4

Sanctified Separation

If you feel an urgency to be part of the company of saints that rises up to meet the challenges posed in the last chapter, then this book is doing what God intended for it. The truth is that the things I am describing are a reality and it is decision time for the Body of Christ. The time has come for a sanctified separation in the Body of Christ. Such a separation will have her rising out of the political correctness that has trapped her like the proverbial frog in a slow boiling pot.

In 2002, the Lord spoke to me in vivid terms about sanctified separation. Right now you may be likening this to separation and divorce in marriage, but that is not what God desires and it's not what He was describing to me. The Lord began to speak to me through Genesis 13 where Abram and Lot parted company. Between them these two men were wealthy both in possessions and herds of livestock, but when their workers began to argue about who was entitled to what, Abram realized the land couldn't support them both. He and Lot agreed to go their separate ways.

So Abram said to Lot, "Please let there be no strife between you and me, and between my herdsmen and your herdsmen; for we are brethren. Is not the whole land before you? Please separate from me. If you take the left, then I will go to the right; or, if you go to the right, then I will go to the left." Then Lot chose for himself all the plain of Jordan, and Lot journeyed east. And they separated from each other (Genesis 13:8-9,11).

The real issue was that Lot was a man of the flesh whereas Abram was a man of faith, called by God with a promise and a mandate. The mandate was clear:

Now the Lord had said to Abram: "Get out of your country, from your family and from your father's house, to a land that I will show you. I will make you a great nation; I will bless you and make your name great; and you shall be a blessing. I will bless those who bless you, and I will curse him who curses you; and in you all the families of the earth shall be blessed" (Genesis 12:1-3).

Abram could not fulfil that mandate or realize the promise while he was with Lot. He had to separate himself. Even though he already knew what land God had promised him, yet he gave Lot "first dibs" to take any part of the country he wanted. He knew Lot was a man of the flesh and would choose the land most pleasing to the natural eye without bothering to consult God. Lot's choice brought him into the vicinity of Sodom where, eventually, he lost everything. The good news is that despite the worldliness of his original choice, Lot was preserved and brought out of Sodom. Even though he was messed up, he was saved. There will be many like him, seduced by the world and caught up in the system, yet they will come out of it and, with repentance, be saved by the grace of God.

While this was a literal event in a specific period of time in the history of the Hebrews, it is also a parable and a prophetic sign for the Body of Christ. Just as Abram had to separate himself from Lot, so the Body of Christ must also come into a sanctified separation. This is not to be a separation brought about by arguments and quarrels, or doctrines and dogma, but will be a separation of flesh and spirit. There are many who are saved because they have confessed Jesus with the mouth, but they do not understand the things of the spirit. They are people of the flesh, influenced more by the ways of the world and led not by the Holy Spirit but by popular opinion. Even many Pentecostals, having once begun in the spirit, are now indistinguishable from the world. On every side there is much disagreement taking place in the Body of Christ. Many believers who are of the flesh are seduced by the pressure of political correctness to compromise with the world. It will separate them from the Spirit.

This separation is already happening as a result of the endorsement of same-sex marriage and the ordination of priests in some streams of the Body of Christ. Metaphorically, I see "Lot" present in the church as a corporate group, and like Lot they will choose to "pitch their tents" in unholy places when they are separated from Abram. A sanctified separation will see many "Lots" going deeper into the ways of the world, while the "Abrams" will pursue the things of the spirit.

The Abram part of the Body of Christ will pursue the promise of an Isaac. Metaphorically, Isaac can represent the harvest of souls. In Genesis 22:17, Abram saw the stars and grains of sand and knew they were pictures of the fulfilment of his faith-seed heritage.

He saw the hope of glory, the seed of Christ Jesus, with multitudes entering the kingdom through the redemptive power of God.

Some people need to "leave the room" in order for the glory of God to break out. This was clearly the case when Jesus was called to the death-bed of Jairus's daughter. He had no hesitation in asking for some members of the family to leave the room. He knew that in order for the child to be raised to life all the cynics, the unbelieving, and the carnal, had to leave. There is currently a window of opportunity for the Body of Christ to be set apart from the world's system. I remember times in my home church, Field of Dreams, when the senior pastor and I would have sought God for hours for a move of the Spirit only to watch people get up and leave when they thought the meeting should finish. But then we saw that it was after they left that the power of God broke out. I mean no disrespect to those who left, but the ones who stayed were the hungry ones, pursuing the things of God, moving in the Holy Ghost, with faith to believe for the miraculous. That was a sanctified separation. It was a smaller, localized version of what I believe is coming to the Body of Christ world-wide.

There has been so much disunity and disharmony in the Body. The divisions amongst us have made us our own worst enemy. Just as in Genesis 13, when the only way to resolve the discord between Abram and Lot was by a sanctified separation, there is a similar need in the Body of Christ, today. Seduced by political correctness, the Lot company will find it difficult not to be caught up in a deranged and demonic world, while the Abram Company will go on to receive its Isaac-harvest in a manifestation of the redemptive power of God. As God's word says, the whole earth is longing for this.

For I consider that the sufferings of this present time are not worthy to be compared with the glory which shall be revealed in us. For the earnest expectation of the creation eagerly waits for the revealing of the sons of God (Romans 8:18-19).

5

Portals with Legs

I was not surprised to read a recent report about a newly formed church called *Way of the Future*. Apparently, its sole purpose is to control the human race through AI and is committed to creating a "peaceful and respectful transition of who is in charge of the planet."[1]

The spirit of anti-Christ has always tried to counterfeit heavenly authority and glorify man. There is nothing new about its intention to replace God and desensitize people to His miraculous power. However, God is raising up a company of believers who will move in an unprecedented realm of the supernatural. God is calling out a company of saints who will pursue the promise, as Abraham did, and move in the spirit and the power of Elijah.

---

1   *https://www.wired.com/story/anthony-levandowski-artificial-intelligence-religion/*

What will this look like? I can tell you now that it's not about tough-guy prayers, or emotional begging. It's about tapping into our God-given inheritance. It's about coming into revelation of our identity and stepping into the Kingdom. The Gospels record John the Baptist as announcing the Kingdom of Heaven with the words, *"Repent, for the kingdom of heaven is at hand"* (Matt. 3:2). In other words, it is as close as our fingertips. It was that close to Nathanael when Philip brought him to meet the Lord.

Philip found Nathanael and said to him, "We have found Him of whom Moses in the law, and the prophets, wrote—Jesus of Nazareth, the son of Joseph." And Nathanael said to him, "Can anything good come out of Nazareth?" Philip said to him, "Come and see." Jesus saw Nathanael coming toward Him, and said of him, "Behold, an Israelite indeed, in whom there is no deceit!" Nathanael [who didn't understand how Jesus knew him] said to Him, "How do You know me?" Jesus answered and said to him, "Before Philip called you, when you were under the fig tree, I saw you." Nathanael answered and said to Him, "Rabbi, You are the Son of God! You are the King of Israel!" Jesus answered and said to him, "Because I said to you, 'I saw you under the fig tree,' do you believe? You will see greater things than these." And He said to him, "Most assuredly, I say to you, hereafter you shall see heaven open, and the angels of God ascending and descending upon the Son of Man" (John 1:45-51).

I imagine Jesus smiling when he called Nathanael *"a real Israelite, [with] nothing false in him"* (John 1:47 GNT). When Nathanael asked, *"How do you know me?"* and Jesus replied, *"I saw you under the fig tree,"* we understand that Jesus had seen Nathanael in the spirit. I would like to suggest that the fig tree was where Nathanael had his devotional times with God, where he found a place of communion in the Spirit. It was where he encountered the Lord. I believe it wasn't the accuracy of the word of knowledge that moved Nathanael, it was him recognizing that he had encountered Jesus under the fig tree in his devotional times. It was a moment of, "it's You!" This caused him to confess faith in Jesus as the "King of Israel."

Jesus then prophesies that Nathanael will see angels ascending and descending to give glory to the Son of Man. In effect, Jesus was prophesying that Nathanael would be among those who would embrace the new order in Christ and be gates within the Gate. *"To them God willed to make known what are the riches of the glory of this mystery among the Gentiles: which is Christ in you, the hope of glory"* (Col. 1:27 NKJV).

I am indebted to my friend and co-worker in the faith, Adrian Beale, who was the one who drew my attention to the fact that Jesus didn't say "descending and ascending," but that "ascending" came first and then, "descending." There is a connection here to the use of sanctified imagination. When we decree the word of the Lord using our imaginations, we start to see the promises of God as a picture. Jesus himself said, *"[the Son] does only what he sees his Father doing"* (John

5:19 GNT). When we start to see the revelation of the Kingdom, we will begin to decree it. And when we decree the word of the Lord in this way, angels will gather because, according to Psalm 103, their primary function is to do the bidding of the Word. *"Bless the Lord, you His angels, who excel in strength, who do His word, heeding the voice of His word"* (Ps. 103:20 NKJV). As we decree the word of the Lord, angels are released. They ascend into the heavenlies to pull the promises of the Kingdom out of the invisible realms and then they descend, interacting with the Holy Spirit to bring them into our physical environment.

Nathanael isn't prominent in the gospels, so it would be easy to treat this story as a sideline; however, it tells us something important. Metaphorically, the fig tree under which Nathanael was sitting represented Israel (Hos. 9:10). Jesus saw that Nathanael was a man tied to the old ways and so He used metaphoric language to explain that a change was coming that would make it possible to experience an open door between heaven and earth. This open door would allow us to draw from the Tree of Life just as was done in Eden—which is what living as a mature believer should look like. In John 10:7-9, Jesus describes himself as the door, or the gate as some versions of the Bible put it. By this revelation we as temples align ourselves with the Eternal Door so that we become a gate within the Gate. Jesus is the Gate within believers who are called to be "gates" between heaven and earth.

This revelation of who we are as ambassadors for the Kingdom of God is going to be a shock to many in the church. It is something many followers of Christ do not yet understand or practice. Such believers are saved by faith in their hearts and the confession of their lips. The grace of God is on their lives, but they aren't aware of how to walk in the spirit. Walking in the spirit results from the intimacy found in being "trees" that are watered by the running stream of the word of the Lord. This is why the psalmist writes:

Blessed is the man who walks not in the counsel of the ungodly, nor stands [submissive and inactive (AMP)] in the path of sinners, nor sits in the seat of the scornful; but his delight is in the law of the Lord, and in His law he meditates [margin: ponders by talking to himself] day and night. He shall be like a tree planted by the rivers of water, that brings forth its fruit in its season, whose leaf shall not wither; and whatever he does shall prosper (Psalm 1:1-3).

We gain further insight into how we can walk in the spirit through the account of Jesus meeting the woman at the well (John 4:7-26). Old Testament law required the Jews to worship God in the Temple, which was located in Jerusalem. The Samaritans had long ago settled for worshiping on the mountain because of their ungodly kings, but now Jesus was explaining to this Samaritan woman that the time was coming when people would worship God in the very courts of heaven itself. In effect, He was saying that access to the presence of God would no longer be through religious rituals or specific places. People would pass through gates of thanksgiving to enter His very courts with praise, as described in Psalm 100. In the spirit it would now be possible to recognize and activate the eternal love of God and come into one-on-one intimacy with the Father.

Woman, believe Me, an hour is coming when neither in this mountain nor in Jerusalem will you worship the Father. You worship what you do not know; we worship what we know, for salvation is from the Jews. But an hour is coming, and now is, when the true worshipers will worship the Father in spirit and in truth; for such people the Father seeks to be His worshipers. God is spirit, and those who worship Him must worship in spirit and in truth (John 4:21-24 NASB).

If we are content to be confined to earth's lower frequency, or atmosphere, our love will be superficial and will struggle to measure up to the eternal God who was, and is, and is to come. When we enter into eternity's atmosphere, or frequency, however, we can govern the Kingdom on earth even as it is in heaven. We become doors, gates, and portals...with legs! This is one of the reasons Jesus taught his disciples to pray, *"Your kingdom come. Your will be done, on earth as it is in heaven"* (Matt. 6:10).

Heavenly Visitation

One time when I was in Hong Kong, I had an experience of heaven. As the apostle Paul said, I don't know if I experienced this in or out of my body, but in this heavenly encounter everything was worshiping. It came in glorious sound waves of love. Even when I came out of the encounter those sound waves stayed with me. You see, when we become "portals with legs," bringing heaven to earth, we will change the atmosphere we live in. When we walk into a meeting, or into a city, the atmosphere will change, and when the atmosphere is changed everything in heaven joins with everything in time, space, and matter to give glory to God.

The atmosphere of Jerusalem changed just before Passover, when Jesus rode into the city on a donkey. Luke records:

> *And as He went, many spread their clothes on the road. Then, as He was now drawing near the descent of the Mount of Olives, the whole multitude of the disciples began to rejoice and praise God with a loud voice for all the mighty works they had seen, saying: "Blessed is the King who comes in the name of the Lord! Peace in heaven and glory in the highest!"* (Luke 19:36-38 NKJV).

The people burst into loud cries of *"Hosanna in the highest! Blessed is He who comes in the name of the Lord!"* (Matt. 21:9). They laid palm fronds at his feet and gave high praise to God. Even the children entered into this extravagant worship. The Pharisees, men of the flesh, were offended because Jesus had brought about a dramatic change in the spiritual atmosphere and opened the way for the entire city to walk through into realms of glory. Because they could not control this, they feared their authority would be undermined. They had put God in a box of their own making and His manifest presence challenged everything they thought they were entitled to.

Some of the Pharisees called out to Him from the crowd to rebuke His disciples. The Pharisees couldn't believe what they were hearing from the crowd. "Don't you hear what the people are saying? Can't you hear their blasphemy?" Jesus answered them with a line taken from Habakkuk 2:11, *"If these [people] should keep silent, the stones would immediately cry out"* (Luke 19:40). He knew that *everything* felt the compulsion to worship because His very presence affected the spiritual atmosphere in the city. He was the gate—the door—to heavenly realms so that earth could join with heaven in giving glory to God.

I am convinced the time is coming when a corporate group of believers will demonstrate Jesus' supernatural authority before world leaders. Scripture describes Daniel in this way, and the Book of Daniel has particular lessons for us in the final countdown to the return of Jesus to planet earth.

We read that Daniel and his friends had great influence with Nebuchadnezzar, a king who was known as the most demonically ruthless ruler of his era. No other kingdom on earth was more powerful, yet the supernatural authority wielded by Daniel showed Nebuchadnezzar that the Kingdom of the eternal God is much greater. Nebuchadnezzar was to find out just how insignificant his authority was, in comparison with the reality of the eternal Kingdom, when God struck him down with madness (Dan. 4:31). He spent seven years in a wilderness of utter powerlessness, even though God allowed his throne and kingdom to be maintained. Eventually, Nebuchadnezzar was converted and restored to his right mind, giving public honor to God.

Similar events will take place in the lead up to Christ's Second Coming. We will see believers empowered to appear before world leaders, just as Daniel was. Such empowerment will be imperative in a world where the increase in technology will counterfeit, and attempt to replace, the power of God. Simulation technology will deceive people into believing they are living in reality. People will be so desensitized to God's supernatural power that they will no longer be able to discern truth from fantasy.

Sanctified Imagination

Separating truth from fantasy is one of the reasons why I teach that your imagination is a very important part of your devotions. Task-oriented prayer has its place, but I believe it is important to ascend into a higher realm with the Lord where we can wrap our imaginations around the promises of God in Scripture. In Psalm 1:2-3, we read that the person who delights in the word of God and meditates on it is like a tree planted beside a stream and will bear fruit in a time of famine. When you allow your imagination to give you a mental picture of that tree and its source of nourishment, you grasp the true depths of its meaning. We will be fruitless unless we are watered by the Word of God.

The sanctified imagination is a facet of scriptural meditation, and as such it is essential for a heart-understanding of the written Word, particularly the prophetic books such as Revelation and Ezekiel. Using your God-given imagination to assimilate the Kingdom of God will bring revelation on the promises, the true scroll, as well as the eternal word of the Lord. As you meditate on the Word, you come into that place of thanksgiving and go through the gates into the courts of praise (Psalm 100). This is how you become receptive to heavenly encounters.

God requires that we be led by the Spirit, *"for as many as are led by the Spirit of God, these are sons of God"* (Rom. 8:14). Sons walk in the authority to govern the Kingdom on earth even as it is governed in heaven. Daniel was one who walked in this authority and the Babylonian kings, Nebuchadnezzar and Belshazzar, honored him for it. They respected his wisdom and integrity. Through being led by the Spirit of God, Daniel brought those proud and powerful men to humble themselves before God. Daniel is a prototype of those who will move in supernatural power to influence leaders and rulers in the days of darkness to come.

Daniel prophesied that knowledge and understanding would be *"closed up and sealed till the time of the end"* (Dan 12:9), but he went on to reveal that when it is time for that unsealing there would be an incremental *"increase of knowledge"* upon the earth. I believe this explosion of knowledge will take place within the next ten to twenty years. With this volcano of technical know-how, Satan will use technology to counterfeit supernatural power and bring great deception. This counterfeit power will have the effect of desensitizing people to the signs and wonders demonstrated by God's people, His church.

However, the raising up of the Elijahs will bring an increase of Daniel-type wisdom which cannot be counterfeited. King Nebuchadnezzar in Babylon, and Pharaoh in Egypt, were quick to recognize that Daniel and Joseph were wiser than any of their own enchanters, magicians, and educated men. In the same way, today's world rulers will come to acknowledge the superior wisdom of Jesus Christ. God's wisdom is beyond the natural, with a supernatural intelligence that springs from righteousness, and demands attention. When wisdom from above is demonstrated, it will reveal the true saints of God and bring a clear separation between supernatural intelligence and artificial intelligence. God's true power will be undeniable.

It is imperative that the Body of Christ be led by the Spirit to embrace the revelation of God's Kingdom. With the increase of technology in this age of iron mixed with clay, those Christians who are of the flesh will have no substance and no ability as agents for change, but those who tap into the gate of Kingdom revelation will see the Presence of God released. The cleverness of advanced technology will convince many people that they are seeing "miraculous" happenings—they may even credit them as coming from God. The enemy of our souls can—and will—exploit that, but he will never be able to imitate the presence and the love of God. As the saying has it: God doesn't have love, He is love. The eternal reality of that is beyond our comprehension, but we can tap into it by faith and release it into the natural atmosphere. As we do that, people will respond to His love even in this end-age of *"knowledge increasing"* and *"running to and fro"* (Dan. 12:4).

When the Body of Christ calls Kingdom signs and wonders from the invisible realms into the physical, and changes the spiritual atmosphere of the natural realms, people will respond to God's presence as never before. Truly, Jesus is the Gate—the Way, the Truth, and the Life. He is the prototype of how we are to walk as men and women anointed and filled with the Holy Spirit. Yes, even as the only begotten Son of God, the prophesied Messiah, He was the model of what we are to be. *"He who says he abides in Him ought himself also to walk just as He walked"* (1 John 2:6). If we claim to know Jesus then we must walk the way he walked. That's not about religious works, it's about living in the revelation that it was God's intention that we do everything Jesus did, and in the way He did it—in the power of God's presence.

In the heavenly encounter I had in Hong Kong, I was standing on the edge of heaven listening to wave after wave of glorious sound. Everything, even the plant life, was worshiping the Lord. Then the waves of sound changed to a melody I recognized and a magnificent male voice began to sing, "I could sing of your love forever." A great lump of emotion rose in my throat, and I was overcome by the awesomeness of the sound of God's love. And even as I was thinking, "I know that song," the Spirit of God said to me, "That song already existed before it came to earth." Immediately, I understood that it was born in the heavenly realms before it was formed in the heart of the composer. That type of worship is integral to changing the spiritual atmosphere. You can tell the difference in a church meeting when a worship leader taps into eternal realms and goes through the Gate in the spirit. The intimacy that leader has with God overflows into the meeting so that it goes to another level in adoration.

Remember what Jesus told the woman at the well? "You don't have to go to the mountain anymore. You can worship in spirit and truth and go straight into His presence, wherever you may be located." In this New Covenant era we are privileged to *be* a gate and also a *carrier* of the Gate, because Jesus lives in us. As we worship we pull the presence of God into the natural realm and alter the frequency in that locality. It is in that changed atmosphere that the genius mind of God can be released to us, and we can receive inventions, songs, art, and also business wisdom and the solutions to all manner of problems, just like Joseph and Daniel experienced.

God's People to Represent His Government

Some members of this new breed may be highly honored, as Joseph and Daniel were, but I see that others will be persecuted for their stand. It is important that no one reading this uses it as license to escape to a desert island bunker with a lifetime supply of canned food. This is not a time for the people of God to descend into doom and gloom and take on a siege mentality. This is the time for God's people to "arise, shine" in accordance to Isaiah 60:1, and to represent the heavenly, eternal government of God. This is a time for God's people to position themselves in places of influence and to actually demonstrate the rulership of Christ. New covenant believers need to grasp this as a revelation. When we come to a place of intimacy with God it is through the gate of worship in spirit and truth; and then the kingdom of God will manifest on earth even as it is in heaven. It is in this changed atmosphere that sinners come to repentance and revival takes place.

An incident in the Old Testament is a dramatic illustration of this. In 1 Samuel, Chapter 10, a company of prophets playing musical instruments came down from a high place to meet Saul, the newly anointed king. The prophets knew their worship would produce a spiritual atmosphere in which Saul could receive an impartation to rule effectively. They understood they had authority to praise everywhere, not only in the tent of the tabernacle, and they knew their worship opened a heavenly gate. Scripture records that Saul was transformed into a different man as a result of meeting the worshiping prophets. *"When they came there to the hill, there was a group of prophets to meet him; then the Spirit of God came upon him, and he prophesied among them"* (1 Sam. 10:10).

In the New Testament, we see Jesus bringing this revelation to everyone. He taught that worship is actually in spirit and in truth, and is not dependent on a specific location. All believers may access the presence of God in spirit and in truth and bring heaven to earth. In this way the very King of Glory manifests in and through His people.

As the eternal Kingdom is revealed and demonstrated by the new breed there will be displays of power even to the magnitude of calling down fire like Elijah the Tishbite. And, just as in the days of Daniel and Nebuchadnezzar, present-day leaders in government will also be influenced to the point of repenting and giving glory to the Most High God.

6

Different Levels of Prophetic Practice

It must be emphasized that the last days Elijah will operate in the role of five-fold gifting. There are many already operating in such gifting, but the numbers will grow as more believers mature into their calling as apostles, prophets, evangelists, pastors, and teachers.

Presently, there is still much confusion in the Body of Christ about what the New Testament says regarding the spirit of prophecy and the "office of prophet." There are a lot of prophetic words released and published on the internet. Most of them are very uplifting, encouraging, comforting, and exhorting for the Body—but that doesn't mean that all of them came from the mouths of people operating in the office of prophet. You can be prophetic without being recognized as a prophet. They are two different levels of prophetic practice.

In an assembly where people prophesy, it is as a result of a corporate Spirit of prophecy that descends in an equipping capacity as one of the nine gifts of the Spirit. 1 Corinthians 12 tells us that the Spirit of prophecy comes on the people so that they may prophesy beyond their natural ability in order to encourage one another.

The manifestation of the Spirit is given to each one for the profit of all: for to one is given the word of wisdom through the Spirit, to another the word of knowledge through the same Spirit, to another faith by the same Spirit, to another gifts of healings by the same Spirit, to another the working of miracles, to another prophecy, to another discerning of spirits, to another the interpretation of tongues. But one and the same Spirit works all these things, distributing to each one individually as He wills (1 Corinthians 12:7-11).

These individual manifestations are gifts for that moment, not giftings that are permanent. People who prophesy in this context are functioning in the power of the Holy Spirit with the intent to edify (or build up), encourage, comfort, and exhort for a specific purpose in that specific time frame. If, in this arena, a word comes as a rebuke or correction in a judgemental sense, it is clearly not from God, because it is not encouraging or comforting.

The second level of prophecy is from the office of prophet. This is a matter of ascending positionally into a higher level of counsel. Scripture tells us: *"When He [Jesus] ascended on high, He led captivity captive, and gave gifts to men. He who descended is also the One who ascended far above all the heavens, that He might fill all things. And He Himself gave some to be apostles, some prophets, some evangelists, and some pastors and teachers, for the equipping of the saints for the work of the ministry, for the edifying of the Body of Christ"* (Eph. 4:8,10-12).

The office of prophet is different from the spirit of prophecy. It is the difference between ascending and descending. The "office of prophet" comes about when a person is chosen by God for that role even before the foundation of the earth. We know this by the way God chose Jeremiah to be a prophet to the nations.

Then the word of the Lord came to me, saying: "Before I formed you in the womb I knew you; Before you were born I sanctified you; I ordained you a prophet to the nations" (Jeremiah 1:4-5).

Today there is a new breed rising up that is chosen just as Jeremiah was. This company knows that the counsel of God brings warnings and—if there is no repentance—it also brings judgement.

There are some who insist that rebuke and judgement have no place in New Testament prophecy, but I disagree. They have not discerned the scriptural difference between the spirit of prophecy and the office of prophet. Jesus Christ, who is not only God, but the prophet of all prophets, sent His angel to John the Apostle with a word for the seven churches (Rev. 2-3). Two of those churches were honored and encouraged, but five of them were rebuked and warned. Remember, this is Jesus of the New Testament; the Jesus who is the same yesterday, today, and forever.

Listen to what He says to the Laodicean Church. *"I know your works, that you are neither cold nor hot…So then, because you are lukewarm, I will vomit you out of my mouth"* (Rev. 3:15-16). To the Church at Pergamos he says He will judge them with the two-edged sword of His mouth if they don't repent of the sin of compromise (Rev. 2:16). He tells the Church at Thyatira that it is entertaining the spirit of Jezebel and, unless it repents, He will be laying on some suffering (Rev. 2:21-23). You can't say that's really encouraging or edifying! But this is Jesus, bringing rebuke and correction because He wants to protect His people.

Another example of warning and protecting in the office of prophet is Agabus.

A certain prophet named Agabus came down from Judea. When he

had come to us, he took Paul's belt, bound his own hands and feet,
and said, "Thus says the Holy Spirit, 'So shall the Jews at Jerusalem
bind the man who owns this belt, and deliver him into the hands of the
Gentiles'" (Acts 21:10-11).

Agabus was warning Paul what would happen if he went to Jerusalem.
It wasn't encouraging but was surely a preparation for what was ahead.

Consider, too, the disciples who were amazing in the operation of the
five-fold giftings. Peter the apostle operated in all five, including the
prophetic. In Acts 5, we see him operating in the governmental role
of prophet to expose Ananias' wrongdoing. And then, in an apostolic
capacity, he rebukes and brings a strong warning, telling him he
has lied to God as well as men. Ananias immediately drops dead.
Three hours later, not knowing what has happened to her husband,
Sapphira ignores the opportunity to repent and tell the truth and she,
too, dies immediately (Acts 5:1-11). Operating in the five-fold gifting,
the apostle Paul took up the prophetic office to denounce Elymas as
a sorcerer (Acts 13:6-12). He harshly rebuked the man, calling him
"a son of the devil and an enemy of everything righteous." Paul
decreed Elymas would be blinded for a time and this demonstration
of power caused the proconsul to believe God. Paul was fulfilling his
mandate to protect and maintain righteousness.

A modern example is that of William Branham. He lost his way regarding some of his teachings toward the end of his ministry, but in his prime he was an accurate prophet in the five-fold gifting. I have heard both Benny Hinn and Kenneth Copeland tell the story of how in Branham's meetings people were given a numbered card to record their requests for healing. A revelatory angel worked with Branham, enabling him to give words of knowledge after calling out a person's number on a prayer card.

Some pastors were convinced Branham was prophesying using details of ailments that were written on people's cards, and one of them conspired to trap him. The card number of this pastor was called out and he came forward for prayer, but Branham discerned that he did not suffer from the multiple sclerosis that was written on the card. Branham told him, "Brother, there is nothing wrong with you," but the man continued to maintain he had MS. Then Branham had a vision in which he saw the man sitting with another pastor and a woman in a green dress. Branham discerned that the man was a pastor in a church in that city. He said, "Sir, you have mocked the Holy Spirit," and pronounced that from then on he would indeed suffer from MS. This proved to be accurate.[1] I remember I was shocked when I first heard this account of Branham's response to that man. How could this be New Testament prophecy? But as I studied the Scriptures, I realized that in this instance Branham was moving in the governmental role of the prophet and that he was exercising the

---

1   *https://www.youtube.com/watch?v=Ot-gRzEWxyQ*
   - Tracy Eckert – Life of William Branham.
   (At 38 min. & 51 sec.)

responsibility to protect the flock. The conspiracy to discredit him could have caused a stumbling block to God's people. It could have caused confusion, especially for the "lambs" of the flock who might have fallen away as a result and ended up in hell. Branham's action was one of governmental authority to bring not only correction, but also rebuke and judgement. God loves his people so much and he will not tolerate deliberate and dishonest attempts to mislead them.

The new breed of the last days Elijah has found a higher place of counsel in discovering its mandate in the prophetic office. It has come to The Gate and become a corporate portal with legs. I am convinced it will move in a high level of counsel in the five-fold giftings, especially in the office of prophet. It will manifest God-given governmental authority and understand that the office of prophet is to adjust the Body of Christ and the nations. It will bring correction, resolve problems, and protect the Body. In protecting God's people, the last days Elijah will bring judgement to the demonic powers who resist those who have a mandate to prepare the way for revival.

7

The Elijah Company

How do we know what the Spirit of Elijah will look like in heralding the return of Jesus Christ to planet earth? The life of the first Elijah, who was Elijah the Tishbite, gives us some clues. Elijah the Tishbite was specifically chosen by God to be a prophetic voice to Israel. This purpose didn't end when Elijah was taken up into heaven, but was handed on and entrusted to Elisha.

Now Elijah took his mantle, rolled it up, and struck the water [of the Jordan]; and it was divided this way and that, so that the two of them crossed over on dry ground. And so it was, when they had crossed over, that Elijah said to Elisha, "Ask! What may I do for you, before I am taken away from you?" Elisha said, "Please let a double portion of your spirit be upon me." So [Elijah] said, "You have asked a hard thing. Nevertheless, if you see me when I am taken from you, it shall be so for you; but if not, it shall not be so," Then it happened, as they continued on and talked, that suddenly a chariot of fire appeared with horses of fire, and separated the two of them; and Elijah went up by a whirlwind into heaven. And Elisha saw it, and he cried out, "My father, my father, the chariot of Israel and its horsemen!" So he saw him no more. And he took hold of his own clothes and tore them into two pieces. He also took up the mantle of Elijah that had fallen from him, and went back and stood by the bank of the Jordan. Then he took the mantle of Elijah that had fallen from him, and struck the water, and said, "Where is the Lord God of Elijah?" and when he had also struck the water, it was divided this way and that; and Elisha crossed over (2 Kings 2:8-14).

Jesus explained Elijah's action of "handing on" to Elisha by telling his disciples that many seeds come from the kernel of wheat that falls to the ground and dies (John 12:24). While explaining that death was the beginning not the end, he was preparing his followers for his own death, but he was also demonstrating that through his death and resurrection, many would be able to grasp the baton held out to them and so become the chosen—as in *"many are called, but few are chosen"* (Matt. 22:14). Like the chosen ones of the Old Testament, it is a choice to step into that intimacy with God to receive the mantle. There are no gurus in the New Covenant era; all may come. Every believer has the capacity to move in the prophetic realm as God speaks to us. Yes, there are significant mandates for specific tasks— *"He Himself gave some to be apostles, some prophets, some evangelists, and some pastors and teachers"* (Eph. 4:11)—but we can all hear from God.

God, who at various times and in various ways spoke in time past to
the fathers by the prophets, has in these last days spoken to us by His
Son, whom He has appointed heir of all things, through whom also He
made the worlds (Hebrews 1:1-2).

Our forefathers used to go to the prophets to hear from God, but under the New Covenant we all can hear from God through Jesus Christ. We all have the same measure of authority that Jesus had. While all of us may tap into the same mantle as the Old Testament greats and fulfil our individual callings, some people in the New Testament era have not understood the distinction between moving in the spirit of Elijah and *being* Elijah. They have fallen into the deception of believing that they are the person—like Elijah—to bring deliverance. The truth is that Jesus Christ has already done that through His death on the cross. I am confident that God is raising up a corporate Elijah; a company of prophets who move in the spirit and power of the original Elijah. This corporate Elijah will not draw followers to themselves in the manner of false prophets, but will lead people to the King of Glory.

It's a common misconception that true and false prophets are determined by their prophetic accuracy. That is not what it's all about. A true prophet may miss it at times; practice and experience must always be taken into account, allowing time for growth in accuracy and anointing. 1 Corinthians 14 instructs us to assess and judge prophetic words and interpretations, but it does not tell us to take out the prophet and stone him if he gets it wrong. Judgement and correction on content is simply the opportunity for a prophet to grow and stay humble. A false prophet, however, is assessed by heart attitude. He may appear to move in power and seem to be accurate in what he prophesies, but if he puffs himself up and allows people to look to him as a guru, he is guilty of elitism and idolatry.

The true prophets of the Elijah Company will not make idols of themselves. They will be more like the icons on your mobile phone apps in the sense that they represent something greater: when you tap on them they will lead you to a much bigger program! A true prophet never forgets who he serves and will always point the way to Jesus Christ, the King of Kings and the Lord of Lords.

We go back to the Old Testament again for insight into the role of this corporate Elijah. In 2 Samuel 12 we see the Lord sending Nathan the seer with prophetic revelation to challenge King David concerning his adulterous relationship with Bathsheba and his murderous plot to get rid of her husband, Uriah. David repents and is forgiven, but there are serious consequences for his actions.

Thus says the Lord: "Behold, I will raise up adversity against you from your own house....For [what] you did secretly, I will do [openly] before all Israel, before the sun." So David said to Nathan, "I have sinned against the Lord." And Nathan said to David, "The Lord also has put away your sin; you shall not die. However, because by this deed you have given great occasion to the enemies of the Lord to blaspheme, the child who is born to you shall surely die" (2 Samuel 12:11-14).

The consequences of David's sin began to manifest among his older children. Murder and sexual sin, including incest, were practiced by his sons, and all of Israel saw it, but the consequences didn't finish with his blood family. As king, David was father to the whole nation, and his personal adultery came to be repeated in the nation's spiritual adultery against the Lord God. The glory days of David and Solomon were well and truly over when the nation embraced Baal worship and rejected the true God. By the time Ahab was on the throne the prophets of Baal were enjoying the patronage of Queen Jezebel, setting up false altars and places of idolatry all across the land. It seemed the national mess was irreversible.

But what did God do? God pushed the pause button! God put a hold on the enemy's plans by sending Elijah the Tishbite. Elijah was a restorer who brought prophetic revelation to the whole nation. He displayed the unmistakable power of God in many signs and wonders, completely shutting down the prophets of Baal. This brought restoration to Israel, destroyed the false prophets, and released from hiding a group of true prophets of God. The nation was saved even on the brink of total destruction.

Some five hundred years after the ministry of Elijah the Tishbite, the prophet Malachi prophesied that God would send another man like him to the nation. He prophesied a second Elijah.

Behold, I send My messenger, and he will prepare the way before Me. Behold, I will send you Elijah the prophet before the coming of the great and dreadful day of the Lord. And he will turn the hearts of the fathers to the children, and the hearts of the children to their fathers, lest I come and strike the earth with a curse (Mal. 3:1,4:5-6).

Malachi's prophecy came during hard times. The Jews had returned from exile and the temple had been completed, but the priests were ungodly and there was famine in the land. The promise of another Elijah to deliver them must have been music to their ears. But, following Malachi's prophecy came another four hundred years of silence; another famine in the lack of hearing the words of the Lord (Amos 8:11). There is no further record of God speaking through the prophets after that—not in dreams, not in visions, not even in angelic encounters—until the day the Lord released a word to a particular priest named Zacharias.

So it was, that while [Zacharias] was serving as priest before God in the order of his division, according to the custom of the priesthood, his lot fell to burn incense when he went into the temple of the Lord. Then an angel of the Lord appeared to him, standing on the right side of the altar of incense. And when Zacharias saw him, he was troubled, and fear fell upon him. But the angel said to him, "Do not be afraid, Zacharias, for your prayer is heard; and your wife Elizabeth will bear you a son, and you shall call his name John" (Luke 1:8-9,11-13).

The angel described how this child would be great in God's sight, being filled with the Holy Spirit even in the womb, and would turn many people back to the Lord. Then the angel announced something even more remarkable:

He [John] will also go before Him in the spirit and power of Elijah, "to turn the hearts of the fathers to the children," and the disobedient to the wisdom of the just, to make ready a people prepared for the Lord (Luke 1:17).

The angel was speaking from the last two verses of the book of Malachi (4:5-6, as quoted above). These words would have been particularly meaningful to Zacharias because at that time Israel was groaning under the Roman occupation. The oppression was physical, financial, and spiritual—and there were no prophets to tell them what to do about it. Those four centuries of silence looked likely to continue into a fifth. Now, suddenly, here was an angel telling Zacharias that the very last message God had given to Israel was about to be fulfilled through a child born to his barren wife, Elizabeth.

God's answer to the nation's cry for deliverance was John the Baptist. He was to be the last Old Testament prophet, a second Elijah coming to prepare the way for the Messiah, the ultimate deliverer. Jesus himself had this to say about John:

What did you go out into the wilderness to see? A reed shaken by the wind? But what did you go out to see? A man clothed in soft garments? Indeed those who are gorgeously appareled and live in luxury are in kings' courts. But what did you go out to see? A prophet? Yes, I say to you, and more than a prophet. This is he of whom it is written: "I send My messenger before Your face, who will prepare Your way before You." For I say to you, among those born of women there is not a greater prophet than John the Baptist (Luke 7:24-28).

John the Baptist's ministry launched a revival of repentance across the nation. Such was the power of conviction by the Holy Spirit of God that thousands came to listen to him and be baptized. There is no record of him moving in signs and wonders, but he did facilitate a revival of conviction and repentance. He himself was a sign and wonder and, as Jesus mentioned, a type of the Elijah who was to come.

8

The Whaler's Inn or Breakfast on the Beach

In the lives of the two Old Testament Elijahs, the Tishbite and John the Baptist, I see a pattern for the corporate Last Days Elijah. Two distinct groups of people are going to emerge; one after the type of Elijah the Tishbite, and the other after the type of John the Baptist, whom Malachi prophesied would be the second Elijah. I recognize, in these two groups, a blueprint of a prophetic cycle of which will take place, corporately, in the days to come.

The members of the first group will follow the pattern of Elijah the Tishbite, who was taken up into heaven. Some of them will end their lives on earth by crossing supernaturally into the eternal realms and not come back. They will be a prophetic people demonstrating God's power, calling down fire from heaven, displaying the righteousness of God, and dismantling false religion and false gods. I see they will move in such a revelation of intimacy and holiness with God that, through them, He will reveal His power to a soaring level. They will give rise to a large awakening which, amongst the western nations, will bring revival before Islam comes into its fullness of world control. When this company of prophets is "taken and is no more," that is when the influence of Islam will gain even greater strength, and darkness will increase on the earth.

At this point the second group of prophets will come to prominence. They will follow the pattern of John the Baptist. They will move in the powerful conviction of the Holy Spirit that will result in a world-wide revival of repentance. The Islamic world will be rocked to its foundations, with many Muslims embracing the revelation of Jesus Christ as Messiah. This will provoke a reaction from the enemy kingdom which will give rise to a wave of persecution that results in martyrdom. But, as with John the Baptist, it will also result in much fruit. It will be the fruitfulness that Jesus described in speaking of His own death and resurrection. *"Most assuredly, I say to you, unless a grain of wheat falls into the ground and dies, it remains alone; but if it dies, it produces much grain"* (John 12:24).

The prophetic company that moves in the power and authority of John the Baptist will produce a tsunami of repentance unto salvation.

As God was showing me this tsunami of repentance, He drew my attention to those believers who had once experienced God but were now caught up with their careers and the deceitfulness of riches.

They gave lip service to God but when things didn't work out for them as they expected they turned their attention to making a way for themselves in the world, losing their focus on Him and becoming distracted by the cares of the flesh.

When anyone hears the word of the kingdom, and does not understand it, then the wicked one comes and snatches away what was sown in his heart. This is he who received seed by the wayside. But He who received the seed on stony places, this is he who hears the word and immediately receives it with joy; yet he has no root in himself, but endures only for a while. For when tribulation or persecution arises because of the word, immediately he stumbles. Now he who received seed among the thorns is he who hears the word, and the cares of this world and the deceitfulness of riches choke the word, and he becomes unfruitful (Matthew 13:19-22).

1 John 2:15-16 tells us this state is the result of *"the lust of the flesh, the lust of the eyes, and the pride of life,"* and instructs, *"do not love the world or the things in the world. If anyone loves the world, the love of the Father is not in him."*

Something similar happened to the twelve disciples. After Jesus' resurrection, they had an amazing encounter with Him in the upper room where he showed them His hands and His side and commissioned them with the words, *"'Peace to you! As the Father has sent Me, I also send you.' And when He had said this, He breathed on them, and said, 'Receive the Holy Spirit. If you forgive the sins of any, they are forgiven them; if you retain the sins of any, they are retained'"* (John 20:21-23). Verse 20 tells us the disciples were glad when they saw, or understood, what this meant, and yet—within days—they decided to go back to their day jobs.

Simon Peter, Thomas called the Twin, Nathanael of Cana in Galilee, the sons of Zebedee, and two others of His disciples were together. Simon Peter said to them, "I am going fishing." They said to him, "We are going with you also." They went out and immediately got into the boat (John 21:2-3).

They had turned their amazing upper room encounter into a temporary, "warm-fuzzy" experience instead of a way of living. Rather than harnessing that experience as an integral part of their lives, they chose to go back to their former pursuits. In other words, they went back to old ways of thinking. But they discovered they were no longer as successful in their old jobs as they used to be.

And that night they caught nothing. But when the morning had now come, Jesus stood on the shore; yet the disciples did not know that it was Jesus. Then Jesus said to them, "Children, have you any food?" They answered Him, "No." And He said to them, "Cast the net on the right side of the boat, and you will find some." So they cast, and now they were not able to draw it in because of the multitude of fish (John 21:3-6).

In dream and vision symbolism, "fish" may represent revelation in addition to being a metaphor for people as fishers of men, but the disciples didn't consider any of this. They didn't even recognize who was standing on the shoreline. They didn't know who this man was when he called to them, "Have you caught anything?" And even when he told them to throw their nets to the other side they still had no idea. They had walked closely with Jesus for three years and yet, in a matter of days, they had become totally insensitive to His presence.

But when they hauled the net up from the right side of the boat, overwhelmed by the abundance of fish, they had a "light bulb moment"; the "penny dropped," as we say in Australia. This encounter brought a fresh revelation of Jesus which was to change their whole way of life. The unbroken nets were suggestive of the new wineskin, and the big catch was a metaphor for the revelation of Jesus Christ, which caused Peter to exclaim, "It is the Lord!" Peter, nearly naked because he was fishing, immediately threw on his outer garment and went over the side to stride out for land, leaving the others to bring the catch ashore. He couldn't wait to get to Jesus. And what is Jesus doing? He is already cooking a breakfast of barbecued fish for them.

So when they had eaten breakfast, Jesus said to Simon Peter, "Simon, son of Jonah, do you love Me more than these?" He said to Him, "Yes, Lord; You know that I love You." He said to him, "Feed My lambs." He said to him again a second time, "Simon, son of Jonah, do you love Me?" He said to Him, "Yes, Lord; You know that I love You." He said to him, "Tend My sheep." He said to him the third time, "Simon, son of Jonah, do you love Me?" Peter was grieved because He said to him the third time, "Do you love Me?" And he said to Him, "Lord, You know all things; You know that I love You." Jesus said to him, "Feed My sheep. Most assuredly, I say to you, when you were younger, you girded yourself and walked where you wished; but when you are old, you will stretch out your hands, and another will gird you and carry you where you do not wish." This He spoke, signifying by what death he would glorify God. And when He had spoken this, He said to him, "Follow Me" (John 21:15-19).

The realization that it is indeed Jesus cooking breakfast for them on the shore causes each one to enter into a new and greater intimacy with Him. They had communion with Him, and like the disciples on the way to Emmaus, it brought revelation. This revelation brought them back into heavenly citizenship; back into that place of relationship with the Father.

Jesus asks Peter, "Do you love me more than these?" The inference is, "Do you love me more than this great haul of fish? Do you love me more than your old ways?" He asks that question three times: "Peter, do you love me?" How lovingly Jesus draws Peter into a public confession and repudiation of his three denials of the Lord outside the High Priest's courtyard (Matt. 26:69-75). How gracious was the Lord in restoring Peter to a position of leadership among the disciples. Then, by repeating the instruction to "feed my sheep," he also re-established and confirmed Peter's calling.

God showed me He will do this for many who, like Peter, have been side-tracked from their true callings. There will be many who will throw off complacency and come out of the religious system to play their part in the great revival that is coming. They will be set apart from the world system, which I believe will be ruled by Islam. Many will be set apart even to the extent of experiencing wilderness in the manner of John the Baptist and the prophet Jonah.

Jonah Takes a Detour

The story of Jonah shows us some parallels for those who will take their place in the Elijah company in the time of revival. Like the disciples after the resurrection, Jonah had a calling from God, but also like them, he chose to run from it to a place of trade. Jonah attempted to escape to Tarshish, which was a land known for its rich mineral deposits. Its people were skilled in smelting and famous for exporting silver, iron, tin, and lead throughout the ancient world. Overcome by fear of God's instruction to prophesy to Ninevah, Jonah sought to hide in this place of worldly activity—and found himself making an unplanned stopover in the Whaler's Inn!

He went down to Joppa, and found a ship going to Tarshish; so he paid the fare, and went down into it, to go with them to Tarshish from the presence of the Lord. But the Lord sent a great wind on the sea, so that the ship was about to be broken up. Then the mariners were afraid; and every man cried out to his god, and threw the cargo into the sea, to lighten the load. But Jonah had gone down into the lowest parts of the ship, had lain down, and was fast asleep. So the captain came to him and said, "What do you mean, sleeper? Arise, call on your God. Perhaps your God will consider us, so that we may not perish." And they said to one another, "Come, let us cast lots, so we may know for whose cause this trouble has come upon us." So they cast lots and the lot fell on Jonah (Jonah 1:3-7).

Jonah knew immediately why the tempest had risen. He stayed in the hold, using sleep to block out the truth—the equivalent of a naughty child squeezing his eyes shut while covering his ears, shouting "lah lah lah lah!" He knew the storm was caused by his refusal to obey God. Eventually he confessed to the terrified crew.

Then the men were exceedingly afraid, and said to him, "Why have you done this" For the men knew that he fled from the presence of the Lord, because he had told them. Then they said to him, "What shall we do to you that the sea may be calm for us?"—for the sea was growing more tempestuous. And he said to them, "Pick me up and throw me into the sea; then the sea will become calm for you. For I know that this great tempest is because of me." Nevertheless the men rowed hard to return to land, but they could not, for the sea continued to grow more tempestuous against them (Jonah 1:10-13).

Finally, in desperation, the sailors took Jonah at his word and threw him overboard. *"And the sea ceased from its raging"* (Jon. 1:15). The Scripture tells us that God prepared a great fish to swallow Jonah and preserved him for three days in its stomach—a miracle in itself—until he was willing to repent. There would be no escape from God. Within the belly of the fish, Jonah began to pray:

"When my soul fainted within me, I remembered the Lord; and my

prayer went up to You, into Your holy temple. Those who regard worthless idols forsake their own Mercy. But I will sacrifice to You with the voice of thanksgiving; I will pay what I have vowed. Salvation is of the Lord." So the Lord spoke to the fish, and it vomited Jonah onto dry land (Jonah 2:7-10).

Jonah being taken to the heart of the ocean is representative of "deep calls to deep," the same words David used to cry out to God in a time of distress (Ps. 42). Jonah going down into the deep was the dark night of his soul that led him to find his identity in God. In that place of enforced intimacy with God he discovered who he was. He knew God's choice of a large fish was no coincidence. Metaphorically, a large fish such as a whale, can represent a large prophetic ministry. Whales are sensitive to frequencies, which may indicate a metaphoric reference to the spiritual sensitivity which is activated in prophets.

At the very time I began to write this chapter about Jonah, I happened to see a report of one hundred and fifty short-finned pilot whales beaching themselves at Hamelin Bay on Australia's western coast. I say "happened" but as discussed in *God's Prophetic Symbolism in Everyday Life* (the book I co-authored with Adrian Beale), God will sometimes draw our attention to a news item, or a natural phenomenon, to illustrate something He wants us to understand in scripture.

In being swallowed by this large fish, Jonah went down into the heart of God to finally accept his instructions and be clothed in his prophetic calling. Then, having accepted this identity, he was released onto the shore, which is a metaphor for being released back into the natural realm. The completed process transformed Jonah into an atmosphere-changer in Nineveh. He was released into the natural realm as one prepared to deal with the evil in that city. A natural man cannot alter the atmosphere of dark places, but Jonah, a changed man, walked into Nineveh, opened his mouth to speak the word of the Lord, and saw that whole atmosphere of darkness transformed. No longer a slave to the system, Jonah could exercise spiritual dominion over it. He was a walking, talking, sign and wonder.

It's tempting to say that Jonah didn't do any of the signs and wonders that characterized so many of the Old Testament prophets, but what greater wonder could there be than a whole city coming to repentance and turning to the Lord God? To be such an atmosphere-changer that even the government officials of the city repented before the Lord, is a sign and wonder to top all signs and wonders. It is comparable to that change of spiritual atmosphere brought about by Jesus entering Jerusalem on the donkey.

The end-times breed of atmosphere-changers will become evident as the Body of Christ goes into a time of transition. At the moment, a lot of western churches are trying to maintain an appearance of having its act together when the reality is that many are backslidden in their hearts. Many are slaves to the system rather than being heirs of the Kingdom. God is calling back those Jonahs who have rejected their original calling and mandate and escaped into business. Don't misunderstand me, God will use business and finance for the Kingdom, but not if you are running from your true calling.

Many modern-day Jonahs reject the call of God on their lives because of religiosity in the Church. They are not necessarily hardening their hearts, or intentionally going off the rails, when they walk away from their calling and turn to trade; disillusionment has made their love grow cold. But God will *restore* these who are perceived as being backslidden because they stopped attending church. This doesn't mean that God says it's okay to avoid fellowship, but rather that it is His heart to give them a fresh revelation of Jesus Christ, the image of God. They will come into the intimacy that activates the Kingdom of God. When they have a renewed revelation of the Lord and his call on their lives, they'll be like Peter and scramble out of that "old boat" faster than an Olympic swimmer!

Just as the darkness of the holocaust preceded the re-birth of the nation of Israel, the turmoil on earth at the present time is the dark before the dawn. We need to see it with hope and excitement. This darkness will inspire followers of Christ to rise up. For many, this will be Joel's *"valley of decision"* (Joel 3:14) to bring in the greatest harvest ever seen on planet Earth. The set apart "Jonahs" will rise like John the Baptist in the spirit and power of Elijah to spearhead a massive revival. A great company of these obedient, sold out followers will transform cities so that millions will come to salvation in Jesus Christ.

This miracle of widespread repentance will not only impact the Islamic establishment but will also usher in the Second Coming of Christ.

9

Decision Time

Those, like Abraham, who separate themselves to pursue the Isaac of promise, will understand what Jesus taught the woman at the well and will have ready access to the Kingdom through worshiping the Father. To live in that Kingdom will be more real to them than what they can see with their physical eyes.

At this point I hope you understand that the Elijah who is coming ahead of the return of Jesus Christ is not one man but a corporate group. I trust, too, that you understand that the historical patterns of the two Elijahs—Eljiah the Tishbite and John the Baptist—will be repeated as a prophetic cycle. The Tishbite was sent by God to be a restorer in a time of apostasy and spiritual adultery that drove believers into hiding. Doesn't that sound similar to our present-day situation? The whole world appears to be in a mess that is too big to fix: Islam is breathing down the neck of Western civilization, idolatry and unbelief contaminate the church, sexual perversion is being taught in schools as legitimate sex education, and political correctness is rampant. With so much of the Church behaving like Lot and walking in agreement with the world, God's people are crying out, "Lord, what is happening to us?"

God will do as He did before. He will send Elijah again, but not as one man. God is raising a corporate body to move in a manifestation of signs and wonders such as the world has never seen. In the face of this display of God's power, people—church and world, alike—will no longer have the luxury of wavering between two opinions. They will have to answer the same challenge the Tishbite put to the people at Mount Carmel: *"If the Lord is God, follow Him"* (1 Kings 18:21). They will have to decide who they will serve. This uncompromising company of prophets who walk in the Spirit, and who know such intimacy in worship, will eventually go through the "gate," just like Elijah of old. They will translate from this realm to their eternal home without experiencing death.

Even before Elijah there was precedence in scripture for this. Enoch also went to God without dying. Genesis 5:24 tells us he *"walked with God; and then he was not, for God took him,"* and Hebrews 11:5 records: *"By faith Enoch was taken away so that he did not see death...for before he was taken he had this testimony, that he pleased God."* This is the historical pattern that will be repeated in the Elijah Company that will be raised up.

I do not name this a "rapture" because that word is embedded in the mindset of futuristic teaching. Futurists believe that a new world order will arise from the Church of Rome and be led by a European anti-Christ. That may well take place, particularly with Islam in the process of taking over Europe, but I cannot subscribe to the futurist stance that every believer will be taken from the earth. Many Christians ask, "Will there be a rapture, or not?" The answer is, yes, there will, but not in the way the futurists teach. I believe a rapture will take place because some believers will have lived in such intimacy with God on earth and will simply not be present any longer. They will be translated, even as Enoch and Elijah were, because they walked with God. But there will be some believers who will still remain on earth.

When God raises the Elijah Company, there will be a season of apparent success in waging war against the forces of evil. But then God will lift His finger off the "pause button" again and there will be a shift in the spiritual atmosphere. This is when the Elijah Company will step fully into the eternal realm. They won't just visit the eternal realms but will cross over and "become no more" in the earthly realms. Having exercised their hearts and mind to meditate on the promises of the Word day and night, their relationship with God will be so intimate that they will literally encounter heaven. The apostle Paul described such an experience (2 Cor. 12), and so did the apostle John (Rev. 4). There are comparable testimonies even in our own generation. The point is that the more time you spend with the Lord, the more you will enter into depths of intimacy, and the more likely you are to access the eternal realms of His presence.

I believe this will happen corporately with the Elijah Company of prophets because they all will be like-minded and in sync with each other and the Holy Spirit. God has always valued and rewarded unity. David likened it to the precious anointing oil that ran down from Aaron's head to the bottom of his priestly garments and released *"a command of blessing, life forevermore"* (Ps. 133:3). With the same thing in mind, the apostle Paul encouraged the people of God to be vigilant to *"keep the unity of the spirit in the bond of peace"* (Eph. 4:3), and to *"be renewed in the spirit of your mind, and put on the new man which was created according to God, in true righteousness and holiness"* (Eph. 4:23-24). It is in the Elijah Company of prophets that the Church will witness the Body of Christ at last coming together in this God-desired unity.

When the first group of the Elijah Company "become no more," God will allow darkness to pick up where it left off. Islam will have even more influence than before, and the enemy will appear to have regained full control. It truly will be a time of great darkness. But this is when the Elijah Company after the pattern of John the Baptist will come to prominence.

A glance back at the Old Testament shows us that when Elisha followed Elijah the Tishbite, God also raised up many other prophets: Isaiah came forth, and Micah. There was Jeremiah, Hosea, Amos and others, all with a particular calling, some to Judah, some to Israel, some to the exiles in Babylon and, in Jonah's case, even to Nineveh in Assyria. Then came the last one, Malachi, who prophesied of another "Elijah" who would prepare the way for the Lord to *"suddenly come to*

His temple" (Mal. 3:1), and *"turn the hearts of the fathers to the children, and the hearts of the children to the fathers"* (Mal. 4:6).

In the person and ministry of John the Baptist we see the fulfilment of Malachi 3:1. This was confirmed at least twice by Jesus. When John sent messengers to Jesus asking if He was the Coming One, Jesus directed them to tell John about the miracles that confirmed the good news He was preaching. Jesus had this to say about John: *"Assuredly, I say to you, among those born of women there has not risen one greater than John the Baptist…and if you are willing to receive it, he is Elijah who is to come"* (Matt. 11:11,14).

Later, after His transfiguration on the mountain, Jesus told Peter, James and John privately, *"'I say to you that Elijah has come already, and they [the Scribes] did not know him but did to him whatever they wished. Likewise the Son of Man is also about to suffer at their hands.' Then the disciples understood that He spoke to them of John the Baptist"* (Matt. 17:12-13).

John the Baptist fulfilled Malachi 3:1, but did not fulfil the prophecy in Malachi 4:6 of *"turning the hearts of the fathers to the children."* That is to be fulfilled by the emergence of the second Elijah in the present era. Only the turning of the hearts of the fathers will turn back the curse that has come on the nations. Truly we could say that our land is under a curse at the present time, with today's generation generally considered to be fatherless—both physically and spiritually. So we see that while John the Baptist did not fulfil Malachi 4:6, he *was* the prototype of the second Elijah Company. This second Elijah Company *will* fulfil it and so prepare the way for King Jesus to return to earth.

When God takes His finger off the pause button, the anti-Christ spirit controlling Islam will rage against the damage done to its spiritual power by worldwide revival. Its fury will unleash a holocaust in which the prophets will be martyred in the same manner as John the Baptist. This is the nature of the spiritual principle of increase. The seed falling into the ground in martyrdom will produce many seeds springing forth to preach repentance. Great honor will be bestowed on them for their obedience in playing their part for the harvest of souls.

And I saw thrones, and they [the saints] sat on them and judgement was committed to them. Then I saw the souls of those who had been beheaded for their witness to Jesus and for the word of God, who had not worshipped the beast or his image, and had not received his mark on their foreheads or on their hands. And they lived and reigned with Christ for a thousand years (Revelation 20:4).

It is apparent that those so honored are raised to life for the purpose of ruling with Christ on earth during the thousand-year reign, because the account continues:

But the rest of the dead did not live again until the thousand years were finished. This is the first resurrection. Blessed and holy is he who has part in the first resurrection. Over such the second death has no power, but they shall be priests of God and of Christ, and shall reign with Him a thousand years (Revelation 20:5-6).

Like Jonah fleeing to Tarshish rather than obeying the call of God on his life, many people give in to fear when God calls them. Some are like Moses who said he wasn't sufficiently articulate in speech to do what God asked. Some act like Gideon who hid in the winepress, protesting he was the least in his family and not good enough for the task. Giving in to fear, they run a million miles in the opposite direction and throw themselves into the pursuit of everything except His call. Very soon, the misdirected fire in their belly stops them from thinking about who and what they have said "no" to. After a while, not even paying lip-service to God on Sundays works for them.

Jonah was the example of what God calls all of us to be in this new covenant era—people who live as a sign to the world. We are all meant to be walking wonders, changing the atmosphere of our city simply by carrying His presence and His word. What greater outcome can there be than hardened government officials repenting and bowing the knee to Almighty God? What happened with Jonah will happen again with the Elijah Company, which even now is being called out to confront the dark rule of militant Islam. Make no mistake, this will be worse than anything the world experienced under Communism or Hitler.

As John the Baptist was set apart to live in the desert, so the end-time Elijah company of prophets will be set apart from the counterfeit religious system that will dominate the world. Like John the Baptist, they will spearhead a revival of repentance and it will be even more dramatic than the one Jonah experienced in Nineveh. The second wave of the Elijah Company will not be translated out of the natural realm like Elijah the Tishbite but will be martyred, as was John the Baptist. Revelation 18 tells us plainly that there will be a great slaughter of the followers of Jesus Christ: *"And in her [Babylon] was found the blood of prophets and saints, and all who were slain on the earth"* (Rev. 18:24).

Revelation 20:4 confirms the martyrdom of followers of Christ who will be beheaded because of their refusal to take the mark of servitude. The multitude of martyrs will gather before the Throne, having been raised from the dead to reign with Christ for a thousand years. These martyrs will be greatly honored in God's throne room and positioned for eternity in the Kingdom of God.

This may seem implausible for today's practices of law. In fact, most western countries have not employed beheading as a means of execution for several hundred years. Britain's last beheading occurred in 1747, while the United States government have never utilized beheading as a legal method of capital punishment.[1] However, in recent years, an alarming number beheadings have taken place under militant Islamic groups, many of which against those who specifically oppose Islam, Christians among them. The fact is, beheading was a standard method of execution in pre-modern Islamic law.[2] And with the alarming increase of Islamic influence in the west, as per Chapter 2, it seems quite probable to conceive this as a movement corresponding to the blueprint laid out to us in end-times Revelation.

1   *https://en.wikipedia.org/wiki/Decapitation*
2   *https://en.wikipedia.org/wiki/Beheading_in_Islam*

10

The Cup is Full

On May 13, 2017, I had a significant spiritual encounter while I slept. It wasn't a dream, but a physical translocation to a Muslim area within Israel.

I knew everything was real and I was physically there because all my senses were active. I was conscious of the smell of food being cooked and the different aromas of the environment around me. My whole body was tense with the sense of danger. All the shops were shut up, and I knew it was because it wasn't safe to be out on the streets.

As I walked through this place, I saw a Muslim woman in labor lying on the roadside. It was obvious she was in trouble. The baby was partly delivered but stuck in a breech position, and I knew that without help both mother and child would die. I had no proper idea of what to do, but there was no one else around so I said "Push," and as weak as she was, the woman began to push. I didn't have any surgical gloves and there was a mess everywhere, but somehow I managed to get the baby out alive. The Lord showed me how to peg the umbilical cord into the belly button and cut it. I had no experience of this in the natural; it was the Lord giving me wisdom. Just when I was about to translocate back, I had a vision within the encounter of the baby growing immediately into a full-sized man who was full of great joy and excitement. I watched this in shock because it was impossible in the natural. At that point I translocated back to my bed.

I was quite overwhelmed and shaken up by this experience; it took me several hours to get over it. But it did take place, and the Lord spoke to me through it. It is a prophetic sign of what is about to happen in Israel.

A baby being born is a metaphor for a promise. A breech birth is a metaphor for problems experienced in bringing a promise to fulfillment. The trauma and near death of this Palestinian mother and her child is a metaphor for the grief, pain, and spiritual death being experienced in the Middle East. The successful delivery against all odds is a picture of the coming revival in that land. Even though many Jews are already coming to faith in Jesus as the Messiah, I believe the breech birth—tail before head—suggests revival will come to the Arabs as a forerunner to the one amongst Jews. The child growing quickly into a man speaks of the maturing of unity in the Body of Christ in Israel, which will result in forgiveness and reconciliation between Jew and Gentile. This revival will be massive.

As I meditated on this encounter the Lord reminded me of Romans 2:8-10: *"Indignation and wrath, tribulation and anguish, on every soul of man who does evil, of the Jew first and also of the Gentile; but glory, honor, and peace to everyone who works what is good, to the Jew first and also to the Gentile."*

With the first coming of Jesus, salvation came initially to the Jews and then to the Gentiles. No one was excluded, but there was an order to it. In the end-time countdown to the second coming, it will be the Gentiles first and then the Jews. I am reminded of the time in 1954 when William Branham, one of God's generals, was on his way to preach in Israel. During a stopover in Cairo, with only thirty minutes until boarding for the last leg to Jerusalem, Branham heard the voice of the Lord saying, "Don't go! This is not the hour." The angel of the Lord appeared to him and repeated, "Stay out of Palestine. This is not your place. The cup of iniquity of the Gentiles is not yet full. There is still more gleaning to do." [1]

That cup is rapidly filling. The Lord showed me that this revival will be the last-day outpouring over Israel, and it's going to happen soon. I also believe that I and many others from the Western world will be drawn to Israel to be part of it. We will see the Holy Spirit completing what He started in Acts 2 with the outpouring in the upper room.

---

1   *Reported in Supernatural: The Life of William Branham. Book 4 The Evangelist and His Acclamation. Owen Jorgensen.*

The rising of the last-days Elijah among both Jews and Arabs will see a surge of opposition to the world of technology led by Islam. It will be the prophesied separation of iron from clay. Despite the growing emotional and physical interaction between humanoids and humans, it will be increasingly obvious that humanoids are unable to interact with the Word of God. Their ability for mechanical and intellectual reasoning will be paramount in their arguments against both the written Word and the prophetic rhema. It is this coldness toward God's word that will reveal the division between man and machine. Those who have spiritual eyes and ears will readily discern the difference.

A Season for Watching and Waiting

Islam's opposition to Israel and to Christianity will increase in the lead up to the Second Coming. Respected Bible teacher Ken Fish, of Kingdom Fire Ministries,[2] wrote an insightful background[3] to the scriptural material I use to explain the Elijah Company's role in the great revival that will lead to Christ's return:

The Abomination That Causes Desolation

By Ken Fish

> *The late seventh century BC was a time of great turmoil in the Middle East. The rising power of Babylon cast a shadow over most of the*

---

2   *www.kingdomfireministries.org*
3   *Used with permission*

region, and any nation that was not already under its sway soon would be. The Kingdom of Israel had been destroyed in 722 BC by the Assyrians (2 Kings 17:6). Miraculously, Jerusalem had survived, but the land and the kingdom itself had been ravaged and weakened by the armies of Sennacherib.

Almost a century passed before Babylon would challenge Assyria for dominance, but around 626 BC Babylon attacked Assyria and by 612 BC even the capital city Nineveh had surrendered. Having wrested control of the known world, Nebuchadnezzar turned his eyes westward. After defeating Egypt, the way lay open for a direct assault on Judah. Among the prizes sought by Nebuchadnezzar were the treasures of the temple that Hezekiah had unwisely shown to Babylon's emissaries after the Assyrian siege (2 Kings 20:12-19; Isa. 39:1-8). Although God had rescued Jerusalem from the Assyrians in direct answer to Hezekiah's prayer (2 Kings 19:14-19,35; Isa. 37:14-20, 36), there was to be no such divine intervention this time. Judah was going into exile for its idolatry, sexual immorality, and treachery.

First, Nebuchadnezzar took into exile many of the nobles in the land. He settled them in various towns and cities within his empire, allowing them to build homes and work the land. Among them was the priest-prophet who was resettled near the River Chebar (Ezek. 1:3). Others, he conscripted into the service of his court, essentially making them Babylonian (Dan. 1:1-4). Among those taken in this way were Daniel and three of his friends. Their age at this time is not recorded, but they were young, possibly still boys, and certainly not out of their teens. As was customary in conquest in those days, they were placed in the care of the chief of the eunuchs, which almost certainly means they were denied their manhood and the ability to father children. In the midst of such sorrow, humiliation, and enslavement, they kept their faith in God (Dan. 1:8).

In 586 BC, on the 9th day of Av (late July/early August), the captain of the imperial guard, named Nebuzaradan, broke down the walls of Jerusalem and the temple was looted and burned. It was a mercy that neither Ezekiel or Daniel saw this calamity. The bloodshed, the rape, and pillage were horrifying. The prophet Jeremiah was witness to these events, writing of them in Lamentations (1:1-4,22). Obadiah also recorded the fleeing Jews' capture by the kingdom of Edom (by then a vassal state of Babylon). Edom not only joined in the pillage of Jerusalem but also formed a barrier to the flight of the Jews, returning them to the custody of the Babylonian armies (Obad. 13-14).

As a high official of Babylon, Daniel would have learned of Jerusalem's fate; he may even have read Nebuzaradan's official report. He would have witnessed Nebuchadnezzar's victory celebrations. In the years following Jerusalem's destruction, Daniel began to have a series of angelic visitations in which he received revelation of the future. The angel Gabriel came at one point to tell him of those kingdoms that would rise after Babylon (Dan. 10:10-21, also see 2:31-43): Persia, Greece, and even mighty Rome. Fourteen years later, Gabriel revealed to Daniel yet another word; a revelatory understanding of the end of times.

At the end of this second visitation, Gabriel unfolded for Daniel a prophetic time clock that has often been overlooked and, even more frequently, misunderstood. He said, "And from the time that the daily sacrifice is taken away, and the abomination of desolation is set up, there shall be 1,290 days" (Dan. 12:11). This passage has sometimes been interpreted by dispensational scholars to refer to the anti-Christ in the end times. It has become one of the defining passages from which the seven-year tribulation is divided into two periods of three and a half years. However, it is unlikely that Daniel would have understood it this way. In fact, as a Jewish exile hearing reports of the fall of Jerusalem, it is likely that Daniel would have understood the abolition of the evening sacrifice to refer to the exact event described above: i.e. the fall of Jerusalem, the desecration and destruction of the temple of Solomon (often called the first temple), and the consequent ending of all sacrifice under the old system. As noted above, this date was the 9th of Av, 586 BC.

Although the Jewish exiles, led by Zerubbabel, Joshua the high priest, Haggai and Zechariah, would later return to rebuild the temple in response to King Cyrus's decree in 538 BC (Ezra 4:6-7), the prophetic timeclock had begun some 48 years before that, on the 9th of Av 586. Indeed, the second temple—built during the return and later expanded by Herod—would be destroyed by the Romans in 70 AD, also on the 9th of Av. This destruction had been prophesied by Jesus from the Mount of Olives shortly before his own death in 33 AD (Matt. 23:37-39; 24:15-24). Since 70 AD there has not been a Jewish temple in Jerusalem.

In biblical prophecy, days are sometimes used as a cipher for years (Num. 14:34; Ezra 4:6-7). If we understand the days of Daniel's prophecy to be years rather than literal days, a picture emerges. If the words that the angel spoke to Daniel are taken literally, that there would be 1,290 days = years from the abolition of the evening sacrifice to the coming of the abomination that causes desolation, then this passage points to the year 704 AD. The math works this way: 586 BC + 1,290 years = 704 AD. Mathematically, we could express that as -586 +1,290 = 704. However, there is no year zero (BC or AD). The counting of years would go minus 1 to plus 1, with the pivotal point being the presumed birth year of Christ. There is some debate as to the exact year of Jesus' birth, but the commonly accepted convention is and was (and the current Gregorian calendar accepts) that when he was born the calendar flipped from 1 BC to 1 AD. Recognizing that there is no year zero means that what calculated out as 704 AD is really 705 AD. This, of course, should lead to the question: what important world event happened in 705 AD that would keep the Temple Mount desolate and prevent either the rebuilding of the destroyed second temple, or the construction of a new, third, temple?

In 705 AD, the Umayyid caliph, al-Walid, completed the al-Qibli mosque begun by his father, Abd al-Malik. This mosque, with its silver dome which has since oxidized to a dark grey, sits at the southern end of Temple Mount and is commonly known as the al-Aqsa mosque, although the term al-Aqsa more properly refers to the entire 14 hectares (35 acres) that comprise the Temple Mount. Included in this complex is the Dome of the Rock mosque with its distinctive golden top, which was completed in 691 AD during the reign of Abd al-Malik. The al-Qibli mosque is the third holiest site in Islam. It was built to commemorate Muhammad's so-called "night journey," in which he was carried from Mecca to the Temple Mount, from which legend says he would later ascend into heaven. The completion of the al-Qibli mosque in 705 AD marked the final major building project of the Umayyids on the Temple Mount.

Although many Jews long for a restored temple (usually called the Third Temple), it is physically impossible to build such a temple due to the presence of the as-Aqsa complex. While some ultra-Orthodox Jews advocate for the building of a Third Temple, to do so would trigger a world war. So long as the al-Aqsa complex stands, the Temple Mount remains "desolate" and without a Jewish temple.

The significance of this fact can hardly be overstated, since the Jewish prophets wrote that the restored Temple would be the site to which all nations of the earth would come to worship YHWH (Obad. 17, 21; Zech. 6:12-13, 14:9, 16-17). Even if the rebuilding of the temple is not necessary for the second coming of Christ to occur, it is necessary for the full and final establishment of the Kingdom of God, with Jesus as its ruler (Dan. 7:13-14 & 27). Of course, the Kingdom of God has a trajectory of its own, and it cannot be stopped (Matt. 13:31-33). This means that eventually something will trigger the removal of the al-Aqsa complex, and the temple will be rebuilt. What and when will that be?

Upon being told about the 1,290 days = years following the abolition of the evening sacrifice, the angel then says, "Blessed is he who waits, and comes to the 1,335 days" (Dan. 12:12). If the convention of a day = a year is maintained, then it appears that Daniel is saying that those who endure 1,335 years after the coming of the abomination that causes desolation, are blessed. Perhaps they are just lucky, because that interval of time leading to the end of the 1,335 years is filled with calamity, difficulty, and upheaval! (Dan. 7:25, Matt. 24:21-22). When will the 1,335 years end? If 1,335 is added to the year of the coming of the abomination that causes desolation, we find that 1,335 + 705 brings the calendar to 2040, which is not far into the future!

What will happen in 2040? The scripture doesn't say exactly, and in fact, Gabriel specifically told Daniel that these matters are shut up and sealed (veiled) until the time of the end (Dan. 12:8-9). 2040 could mark any number of significant events: for example, the rebuilding of the temple (either its beginning or its completion), the coming of the anti-Christ, or perhaps even the return of Christ. The scripture doesn't tell us, but it makes it clear that 2040 is significant in the prophetic timeclock. Many have stumbled into error by attempting to state the year of Christ's return. The day and hour of His coming is unknown to all but the Father (Matt. 24:36), so this article specifically disavows any claim as to when Jesus will return. Could Jesus return in 2040? Of course, He could, but He could also return before or after that. What is clear is that something significant is pending in 2040, and it will have worldwide and perhaps even cosmic implications.

These are momentous years, and many things which have been hidden through the ages will come to light. Due to the presence of the al-Aqsa complex, Islam presents a barrier, but not an insurmountable one, to the return of Christ. Taking the teaching of the Jewish and Christian Scriptures seriously—specifically that the Messiah will return through the East Gate which faces the Mount of Olives (Zech. 14:4-5)—the Waqf that governs the al-Aqsa mosque long ago sealed the East Gate of the Old City of Jerusalem and made the land outside that gate a Muslim burial place. Their reasoning was that the Messiah would not be willing to enter the City by crossing desecrated ground! It would appear the Islamic community takes the teaching of the Scriptures more seriously than most Jews or Christians. Additionally, the Scriptures promise that many will be gathered from among all nations (Isa. 56:3-8), and those nations will include those that traditionally have been considered Islamic lands. Jesus loves Muslims! This is a season of watching and waiting, and the next two decades promise to be momentous. While the Church watches and waits, she can and should pray, as she has in centuries past, "Maranatha!" Even so, come Lord Jesus!

Summary

The prophesied gathering has already begun, with many Muslims experiencing documented dream and vision encounters with Jesus Christ. Before his death in 2014, the respected prophet, Bob Jones, prophesied a billion-soul harvest that would include the

Muslim world. Muslims are being prepared for further revelation and inclusion in the coming great revival. The billions coming to salvation in Christ will confound Satan and his agencies, and reduce them to impotence. Satan's fury will rage against the saints, but with the rising of the Elijah company, the people of God will set their foreheads like flint, and will be unstoppable.

11

Called to Carry Revival

Do I hear you saying, "I'm a little overwhelmed right now, Adam? I'm not sure how this relates to me. How am I going to move in the spirit of Elijah?" I encourage you to keep in mind that the end-time Elijah is a corporate body of people. Individuals will take their place and play their part, but they will be seen in a glorious oneness; a united expression of God's love and power to change the world.

Many will operate within the market place: the world of business, fashion, hospitality, construction, entertainment, and sport; others may come from professional areas such as education, law, or medicine. Some may have a major platform—for instance, in teams for crusade evangelism—but most will be solid, faithful believers. There are as many expressions of destiny and calling as there are people, but as we come together in a body we will all move in the realm of a powerful anointing. The Spirit of Elijah will be about evangelism in many different forms and will be accompanied by signs, wonders, and miracles. Everyone can carry revival.

The revivalist, Evan Roberts, who was prominent in the 1904–1905 Welsh Revival, was a man who sought God. He didn't have a big-name ministry, but he did have a vision of the nation being lifted up into Heaven. He was constantly in prayer, positioning himself in The Gate, Christ Jesus. Because he walked in a realm of glory, all of Wales was changed.

The outpouring that operated through Evan Roberts had a domino effect on churches and the wider community. True reformation took place. Hotels became houses of prayer instead of places to purchase alcohol. Prostitutes were born again and turned the brothels into venues for home fellowship. When people came to their doors expecting the usual houses of ill-repute, they came under strong conviction, becoming born again and transformed. Major sporting events were canceled because of the revival that was taking place. All of this happened because one man positioned himself to become a gate. He was a true revivalist in the Spirit of Elijah, bringing the hearts of the fathers and children to each other, and carrying the anointing and authority to lift the curse off Wales.

My friends, how hungry are you to see the lost coming out of darkness and receiving a revelation of Jesus Christ? Winning souls begins with ministering individually, one on one, but too many Christians are caught up in criticizing what other people are doing or not doing. If only they would put all that energy into winning souls! I am convinced that revival begins as one-to-one and the Western church needs to grasp the power of that. I'm aware of churches who do evangelize, but all too often what is called church growth is nothing more than people moving from one church to another.

I recall a gentleman asking me, "You call yourself a prophet. What spirit are you of?" I replied, "Well, I'm of the spirit that led eighteen people to Christ this weekend. Can I ask how many people you have led to Christ this year?" To his credit, the man apologized and confessed, rather sheepishly, that he had never led anyone to the Lord. There are over two billion Christians in the world. If this week, each one of them led just one person to Christ, that would be two billion people born again. We would have a revival on our hands. The devil would be in a fetal position, sucking his thumb!

In 2003, I was praying with a group of leaders and intercessors. At that time, I was recognized as a prophet but I didn't have a platform for ministry in the local church. As we prayed, I had a bizarre vision. Now, you only have to read the book of Ezekiel to know that God can show us some very strange things, so please don't misunderstand or be offended by what I'm about to describe. In the vision, I saw a naked and bleeding man, having had his genitals ripped from his body. Genital organs, of course, represent the ability to reproduce. I knew immediately that this represented the Body of Christ, the Church, with evangelism removed from it. I told the people I was praying with that the Lord was concerned that evangelism has such a low priority in the Western church and that there is little sense of urgency for winning souls. This did not go down well with those leaders. Their attitude indicated that they would have liked to turn me out!

When it comes to winning souls, while it's true that things like public street preaching has its place, I really do believe that the key to true and effective evangelism is building relationships with people. Daniel had a relationship of trust with the leader of the eunuchs, who was charged with training the young Israelites to serve in the palace (Dan. 1:1-9). This relationship paved the way for Daniel to speak into King Nebuchadnezzar's life. Joseph found favor with Potiphar which, despite the actions of Potiphar's wife, eventually led him into a connection with Pharaoh. Building relationships with people gives us a platform that enables us to share the truth of the Gospel with them. As we build relationships, people will trust us, and that primes their minds and hearts into willingness to listen to us.

Dream Interpretation as a Tool

Dream interpretation for evangelism is a powerful aid to building relationships. In the past, I have evangelized with a small team at "Body Mind Psychic Expo" and other psychic fairs. At the time, this upset some Christians who considered I was in danger of "catching a demon" by attending such events. They appeared to think being demonized is accidental and random, like catching a cold from being in the same room as someone who sneezed! But we are told to be the light in dark places (Matt. 5:14-16) and *"greater is He who is in you [us]"* (1 John 4:4 NASB). Believe me, when we take the light into these places, the cockroaches scatter!

We put up a sign saying, "Free Dream Interpretation," and people lined up. We were bold in God to say that if nothing happened they were entitled to complain to the organizers of the Expo. We were able to tell them what their dreams meant and what God was saying to them. The interpretations always pointed them to Jesus. Most people would exclaim in amazement, "This is exactly what's happening in my life!" When we asked if they would like us to pray for them so they would encounter the Spirit from God, there were very few refusals. When we laid hands on them and prayed nearly every person would react in some way and say, "What was THAT!" We told them it was the Holy Spirit who is actually the Spirit of Jesus. After that it was not difficult to lead them to Christ.

Obviously, they needed to hear the principles of the Gospel such as the need for repentance, but it is much easier to explain these things when there is a relationship of trust and credibility. In the Old Testament, Joseph and Daniel used dreams and visions in their dealings with non-believers. On the day of Pentecost when the gathered believers were filled with the Holy Spirit and astonished the multitude, Peter told them:

And it shall come to pass in the last days, says God, that I will pour out of My Spirit on all flesh; Your sons and daughters shall prophesy, your young men shall see visions, and your old men shall dream dreams (Acts 2:17 NKJV).

Dreams and visions are tools that every believer can use in evangelism.

In the course of ministering together, my friend Adrian Beale and I had the privilege of meeting James Watt, who was the last remaining elder of the Latter Rain Revival in the USA. Before he went to be with the Lord in 2014, we visited him in Seattle, and he was pleased to endorse our book *The Divinity Code: Understanding Your Dreams and Visions.* Adrian and I were thrilled to hear his first-hand accounts of the 1948 Healing Revival during which he sat under the ministries of both William Branham and Oral Roberts. He endorsed our book because, during a visit to Israel in the 1990s, the Lord appeared to him in a vision and told him that dream interpretation was one of the keys to the end-time outpouring for harvest.

I want to encourage you to use your authority in Christ to interpret dreams and visions. As recorded in the Book of Acts, the New Covenant era began when the mantle of Jesus' authority was received by His followers. In his powerful sermon in Acts 2, Peter was quoting the prophet Joel when he said, *"And it shall come to pass in the last days, says God, that I will pour out My spirit on all flesh; Your sons and daughters shall prophesy, your young men shall see visions and your old men shall dream dreams"* (Acts 2:17). Jesus Christ, who is Himself the very spirit of prophecy (Rev. 19:10), is the same today as he was in Joel's time and in Acts 2.

The Spirit of Elijah is unapologetically prophetic and moves in signs and wonders for revival evangelism. When asked, people readily admit to being interested in what their dreams mean. Dreams and visions are great evangelism tools that enable us to minister equally effectively to people from *all* walks of life; from kings and presidents, to people in the street, and even to your family. Don't be intimidated or discouraged by your family and friends resisting the gospel. Ask the Lord for interpretation of their dreams. Never give up on those unsaved loved ones. Not even the most stubborn of them.

12

Stewarding the Call

When I see a mantle of the prophetic over someone I'm praying for—during a conference, for instance—I don't announce, "You are a prophet!" Rather, I've learnt that it is better to describe what I see as an invitation that the person can grow into. In much the same way the Spirit of Elijah also begins as an invitation.

When we begin to hear God, He always starts by speaking into our personal lives. It is as Jesus instructed: first take the plank out of your own eye before you attempt to deal with the splinter in someone else's. If God is going to use us, He will always discipline us, just as a good father does with a loved son (Heb. 12:5-7). Even Jesus, knowing full well he was to "be about the Father's business," spent eighteen years being trained for it. God brings correction as well as encouragement. And His sheep hear what He has to say, *"My sheep hear my voice, and I know them"* (John 10:27). This discipline has no bearing on our salvation or eternal life, which is a free gift that comes through Calvary. But discipline is applied so that we will grow up and mature into our calling. This is necessary whether our level of mandate is small or great. Discipline is so important, because it shapes character. We don't want to be ones who muddy the waters by misrepresenting the Lord with immature behaviors. We want to be good representatives of His kingdom and not cause anyone to stumble.

So, we accept the Father's discipline, we come to a level of maturity, and then we are ready to prophesy in corporate settings when the Spirit of Prophecy descends on the congregation. As part of a local congregation, we can exercise our prophetic giftings under an umbrella of protection in a safe place. This is a process by which we gradually build a two-way relationship of trust. People start to recognize our gifting to edify and encourage, and God can begin to promote us. Trust comes with building relationships in the Body. There is no place for would-be prophets going from church to church and hijacking the microphone with "thus says the Lord!" People will recognize the gift on your life when you have a two-way relationship with your leaders and you honor accountability.

For some, this has proved to be easier said than done. People come to me saying, "My pastor doesn't recognize the things of the Spirit." If you find yourself in that situation, you will need to find fellowship with people who are of the same spiritual DNA. The disciples met together in one mind when the Spirit came with a mighty wind and tongues of fire. You need to find a congregation where you can be in agreement with the leadership. This is essential if God is to raise you up in ministry to the church. Only then can you move from prophesying encouragement under the Spirit of Prophecy to taking up a five-fold gifting as a watchman on the wall with an anointing to bring protection, correction, and judgement. It may be that you move into the office of prophet through being part of the leadership as an elder, but everything will have started with God first speaking into your personal life.

When you have credibility within the local church, you will start to have an effect in the market place. As I did, you might begin as an evangelist with a prophetic edge. You might find yourself with opportunities to minister to high level business people. Together with my good friend Todd Weatherly, I once ministered to some business executives in the Bank of China, and God opened the door to prophesy into their lives. When some of them came to the Lord, I then had the opportunity to step into the office of prophet to bring a governmental level of correction, with solutions to the problems they were experiencing.

There was an occasion when Adrian and I were ministering at a conference in New Zealand and a particular gentleman came forward for dream interpretation. As Adrian finished interpreting his dream, the angel of the Lord came to stand with me and enabled me to release an accurate word over the man. Afterward, the pastor of the church said, "Did you realize you were ministering to the Mayor of the city?" In our B & B accommodation the next morning, as soon as we turned on the light there was an immediate knock on the door. It was the mayor and his son-in-law. They had been waiting for us to wake up. We ministered to them with dream interpretations and prophetic words, and the son-in-law was moved to tears by the power of God. That evening we went to dinner with them and we had great favor to speak into their lives.

There are always opportunities for God to speak to us in marketplace situations. God is waiting for us to use prophetic gifting in this arena, in both the descending Spirit of Prophecy and the ascending office of prophet. Evangelism in conjunction with the prophetic is powerful.

Cooperating with Holy Spirit

I didn't have a personal experience of Jesus until the '80s, but my upbringing in a Catholic family had caused me to believe in God. I enjoyed long discussions with my best friend, Fergus, but any time I raised the subject of God he pretty much talked me down. His parents were highly educated medical professionals and the whole family was very intellectual, so I was always the loser in any debate with him. This was very intimidating for me, even though we were good friends. We continued to have discussions about God after I was born again, but he still out-talked and out-reasoned me.

Meanwhile, Fergus' mother, who liked me and trusted me in preference to some of his other friends, became ill and was dying with cancer. One night the Lord spoke to me and told me to go and pray for her. He made it plain to me that she needed to receive Jesus before she died. I was overwhelmed by this instruction. How was I going to lead this woman to Christ, especially in the presence of her clever husband plus Fergus and his intellectual brothers? I was utterly intimidated.

Such was my fear of man that I put off going to see her. I had all the arguments: She's not going to receive Christ. No one in that family believes. What hope do I have of success when I can't even win an argument with Fergus? She passed away before I mustered the faith to speak to her.

At her funeral, at a tiny cemetery in the foothills of my home city, Fergus' older brother came forward to speak and what he had to say shocked me. He said, "I'm really proud of my mum, because she was a Christian and she gave it all up for my Dad. Most people wouldn't be that brave. Good on you, Mum!" I was shattered. Now I understood why God wanted me to speak to her and pray for her. I had failed them both.

Fifteen years went by and Fergus told me about a black spot on his tongue. I urged him to have it checked out with his doctor, but he didn't. Eventually it was diagnosed as cancer. He had part of his tongue removed, but it quickly spread to his throat and lungs, and his condition was pronounced terminal. My best friend was dying, and I was confronted with the same challenge I'd faced with his mother. I knew I had to speak about Christ to him, but now there was the additional problem of living 1,000 miles (1,600 kilometers) away from each other. I couldn't speak with him face to face.

As I considered how to deal with this, I had a vivid dream encounter. I found myself underground in the chambers of hell, watching demons preparing to confine people for torment. A dreadful torment was being laid out. I knew a river of molten lava would pour through this place to burn them all. And I knew one of those chambers was for Fergus. Immediately, I booked a flight to visit him in hospital.

I can't describe how awful it was to see my friend hooked up to all manner of tubes and struggling to breathe. As I was sharing the gospel, I explained to him how simple it is. The gospel is a gift, not a reward. John 3:16 is all about God's love in giving His only begotten son. That love is real. As I was telling Fergus this, his eyes began to tear up. I thought this was a good sign, that he was softening to the gospel. But through his tears, he said, "Adam, I'm sorry. I can't do this. I appreciate you and love you, but I can't believe. I'd only be doing it for you." I was devastated. My best friend had just rejected Christ, and I had seen the place of torment that was being prepared for him.

The next morning, I was with him again before catching my flight home to Adelaide. I hugged him, knowing it was the last time I would see him. All I could think of to say was, "Fergus, if it gets really scary right at the end, can you promise me you will at least consider accepting Jesus as your Savior? All you have to do is call on the name of the Lord. Scripture says that he who calls on the name of the Lord will be saved." Tears ran down his face and, surprisingly, he nodded his head.

A few weeks later, I was preparing for a trip to the US. On the eve of departure, my wife, Paula, received a call from Fergus' wife: "Fergus is in and out of consciousness now. He came out of it and asked for Adam a couple times." When I phoned back, I was told Fergus was sleeping and she didn't want to disturb him, but she promised to have him call me as soon as he woke up. I knew how important it was to speak to him immediately. I urged her to wake him, but she wouldn't, even though I told her I knew what he wanted to talk to me about. All through the night I was praying. I couldn't sleep while I waited for his call.

Finally, at five in the morning, Fergus' wife called to say that he had passed away. Once again, I was shattered. All I could do during that long thirteen-hour flight to Los Angeles was to fix my eyes on the Author and Finisher of my faith.

Some months later, Fergus' wife and sons were in Adelaide to visit his family, and Paula and I invited them to dinner. They raised the subject of Fergus' "weird" behavior just before he died. I asked if they knew what he had wanted to say to me. This is what they told me: "Tell Adam I'm going to be okay. I did it. My mum's with Him and they're waiting for me."

I was so relieved, I wept. Fergus' family didn't understand my tears, so I told them exactly what I told him: whoever calls on the name of the Lord will be saved. I explained how Fergus and I used to have debates about God, and how I used to pray for him and how he always rejected that. As I shared these things, she—and her sons too—became teary. It was a very emotional time for us all. I was privileged to lead them all to Christ, and to pray for them. Perhaps you have questions about loved ones who have passed away. You may wonder where they are now. Are they in heaven? Are they with you, Lord? Let me encourage you not to look on the natural circumstances. Don't be moved by the lies of demons who operate in fear and doubt. God wants us to be moved by every word that proceeds from the mouth of God.

I have prayed for many people and have witnessed many miracles: a woman who was pronounced brain dead coming out of a coma and having their funeral canceled, the curse and effects of Hepatitis C broken off, Parkinson's disease completely healed so that the man could walk normally, and countless more. God is not—I repeat—He is not the author of cancer or any other disease, but in these circumstances He may use it so that people will take their eyes off their own mortality and look to the Immortal One, Jesus Christ. He allows it so there is an opportunity to call upon the name of the Lord and be saved.

I want to encourage you not to give up on your loved ones, no matter how they may talk you down. Do not be intimidated into not believing for their salvation. God wants us to fix our eyes on things above, where Christ is seated. He wants us to position ourselves as gates within the Gate, even as Evan Roberts did. Don't be moved by what you see with the naked eye. He wants us to speak into the spiritual realm beyond natural circumstances, so that we change the spiritual atmosphere of our family, neighborhood or even city, as Jonah did. As the spiritual atmosphere is changed, the anointing comes. Even as you are reading this, the Spirit of Elijah is coming upon you.

A Higher Level of Authority

Once you are ministering freely in the marketplace as well as to friends and relatives, then God can bring you into a higher level of speaking to people in authority. From there you may become a prophet who releases a word for nations. When you are faithful with small things, God can entrust you with greater things. He will give you downloads at a higher level. One of the earliest examples of this in my own life was when I was ministering in Papua New Guinea. I was introduced to some members of parliament and, in the course of conversation, God gave me a word for the nation. However, at that time, local church politics were such that I was prevented from releasing it personally to the Prime Minister. Then I was invited to a corporate lunch with the Prime Minister, which led to the invitation to release the prophetic word on the government-run radio and TV stations.

In 2018, the Australian Government was experiencing bitter infighting and undergoing a leadership challenge. Unbeknown to me, there were many Christians praying and fasting for this situation. At 4.30 a.m. on September 2nd, the Lord woke me up with a vision of a foot in a doorway, preventing it from being shut. Then I saw someone walk through the doorway. The Lord told me, "Tell my people to pray for the next election."

Immediately, I understood that with the elevation of a born-again, committed Christian to the leadership of the party that held power, God had indeed placed a "foot in the door" to hold back unrighteousness in our nation. But I knew the opportunity could be short-lived. Within months, the nation was due to go to the polls in a Federal election and the opposition party had already indicated it would change the existing laws on religious rights if it won the election. The door would be closed on freedom of religion.

The foot in the door was the opportunity for God's people to pray as never before. It was also a warning that if this godly Prime Minister's government was not re-elected a great darkness would come over the nation. The spiritual forces behind political correctness and left-wing ideology would have free rein to promote perversion and persecute the Body of Christ. How true is 2 Chronicles 7:14: *"If My people who are called by My name will humble themselves, and pray and seek My face, and turn from their wicked ways, then I will hear from heaven, and will forgive their sin and heal their land."*

The Lord had me release this foot-in-the-door vision at a Sunday meeting where I was ministering, and then gave me two further words in relation to it. First, He said, "Revival *will* come. It's not if but *when*, but it can come the easy way or the hard way." Not only has revival been prophesied over Australia as the Great Southland of the Holy Spirit, but also God wants to complete the blessing that resulted from the World War I Australian Light Horse troops liberating Jerusalem after defeating the Ottoman army at Beersheba.[1] That prophetic sign of the blessing on Australia will culminate in the greatest revival the world has ever seen. Second, the Lord made it very plain: it's either prayer or persecution. We have been warned.

Four days later, an article appeared in national media in the political section of *The Guardian*. The headline read: "Pentecostal leader claims darkness will come if Scott Morrison not re-elected." The article was reprinted by the premier daily newspaper, The Australian, and was subsequently reported in Chinese, British, and American media. The result was the release of the "dogs of war" and I began to receive a barrage of hate mail. Praise God for his canopy of protection over my life!

---

1   *See DVD feature documentary **Arise**, Phillip Fraser and Elizabeth Fraser.*

The demonic reaction to the "foot in the door" word was a compliment, because God showed me some time ago that there are two indicators of whether or not you are operating in the office of prophet. The first is that the word you bring will become public and well-known in the "city," that is, nationally. Secondly, it will stir up the Jezebel spirit which will attempt to intimidate you with the express intention of discouraging you and shutting you down. But God will protect you. He will never allow the Jezebel spirit to destroy you.

The word about the foot in the door was to warn and protect the Church. I released it for that reason. The function of the office of prophet is always to bring solution to problems and to bring warning of judgement if there is no repentance. Ultimately, it is all about souls coming into God's Kingdom. Corporately, the Church of Jesus Christ is being positioned as a beachhead, empowered to evangelize, bring repentance, and usher in the Spirit of Revival.

13

The Invitation

Many people boast, "I don't believe in God," but the fact is they *do* believe in something. Everyone has some form of an idol they worship. It might be sport, reputation, or a bank balance. It might be another person, such as a wife, husband, lover, or child. Many people try to live their lives through their children. Driven by their own goals and unfulfilled promises, they become obsessed with their child's success. That is idolatry, because whatever drives us becomes our god. I hope that statement challenges you to have a bigger perspective, with your eyes fixed on eternity and the Kingdom of God, rather than short-term desires.

In 2007, during my own journey to take up God's invitation to fulfil my mandate, I had the following encounter with Him:

In this encounter, I knew that I had already lived for over a thousand years and my wife, my friends, and my sons had already passed into eternity. During this experience I remember sitting with my daughter who appeared to be in her nineties. I held her hand as she, too, slipped into eternity. I remember feeling the tears running down my face and tasting the salt of them. In a series of encounters, I also saw this happening with my children's children and their children's children. I felt so lonely. I would establish new relationships, new friendships, but the cycle would keep happening, again and again, through the generations. I felt life was meaningless without the close relationships of family and friends. Ecclesiastes 1 came to mind, of how pointless, how futile, life is. Solomon obviously experienced this sense of pointlessness when he wrote that *"all [people] are from the dust, and all return to dust"* (Ecc. 3:20). Then I saw how foolish it was to feel like that. I recognized how often it is that we build relationships primarily to cater for our own insecurities; to be accepted by people and have their approval. Still, in the encounter, the years passed by. My knowledge expanded and my wisdom increased. It was though the world was a bubble I was peering into. I learned how important it was to build relationships that reflect Christ, and have the impact of leading people away from the gates of hell and into intimate relationship with the Eternal God. This, in turn, further opened my eyes to the greatness of God's love. Jesus, the only begotten Son, laid down His life so that humanity could live eternally in relationship with the Father. Although God allowed Satan to influence us, He used even that to demonstrate His love in sending light into the darkness. I heard, "Do you love me more than these loved ones?" and I remembered Christ's words to Peter at the beach breakfast.

I had come to the realisation that I could no longer allow anything to come between God and me.

Following that encounter, I accepted that there's nothing inherently wrong with taking pleasure in enjoying life and our earthly relationships—life is meant to be beautiful and abundant—but the experience showed me it's important to have our sights set on the big picture. With that in mind, I want to draw upon three more encounters. They are not my own, but they illustrate God's invitation to His people and His determination to fulfil what He has written on the scrolls of nations. These encounters demonstrate how the prophets are rising up, even in our own time, to carry the flame from previous generations. They are seeds falling into the ground to bring forth more fruit.

The first concerns Arthur Burt, shared to me by my dear friend Kathie Walters,[1] who knew Arthur very well and often visited him. Arthur Burt was a man who was part of a move of God, in Wales, in the early part of the last century. In 1930, Arthur was a member of a Pentecostal group in which a powerful end-times word was prophesied. Although he carried a written record of this prophecy until his death in 2014, he had never before shared it with Kathie.

On returning to USA, Kathie had occasion to telephone the prophet Bob Jones. Bob didn't know anything about Arthur Burt at that time,

---

[1]   *Used with permission*

but he discerned Kathie had just visited an elderly man in Wales. Bob said, "Tell him he will see the word come to pass. Everyone else who heard it is dead, but he will see it."

Kathie telephoned Arthur to ask what the word was and also pass on what Bob had said about it. This is the word which Arthur had carried on his person for years, in the form of a written letter:

"There shall come a breath and the breath shall bring the wind and the wind shall bring the rain and the rain shall bring the floods and floods and floods, and the floods shall bring the torrents and torrents and torrents. So shall they be saved, like falling leaves from the mighty oaks swept by a hurricane in a great forest. Arms and legs shall come down from heaven and there shall be no ebb."

Bob Jones, speaking at conferences in 2009 and 2011, connected Arthur's word with his own encounter (which he had been carrying since 1975) concerning the billion-soul harvest. He explained that floods are movements of the Lord, and that torrents had to do with end times revival and the billion-soul harvest. A torrent is a river in extreme flood that cannot be stopped. Arthur's prophecy was received in 1930, the very year Bob Jones was born. God was laying down a series of prophetic "stepping stones" to unfold to His people what was coming. *"The Lord God does nothing, unless He reveals His secret to His servants the prophets"* (Amos 3:7).

On Valentine's Day, February 14, 2014, in Texas, a prophet (who prefers not to be named publicly) had a spiritual encounter. Only later did she learn that Bob Jones had died on the very same day. I see this as another stepping stone in the unfolding revelation of the end-time revival to come. The account was told to me by the prophet, digitally voice-recorded and later transposed as follows:

In this encounter, all my senses were activated, as in a physical experience of what was happening. I was there! I saw the Lord. I was so conscious of His eyes. They were so beautiful. In them I was aware—I could see—how He felt about me. All I wanted to do was praise Him. I didn't want to stop! I was standing on a circle of snow as I looked into His eyes. I saw myself reflected in His eyes, but I also knew He saw himself in mine. I understood this without any words being spoken. It was such a beautiful witness to complete one-ness— the wholeness of why He created me. There was so much joy in this wholeness that I just whirled and danced on that circle of snow.

I was aware it was the last second before His return. It's hard to explain, but I didn't have to be told this. It was simply that He allowed me to have the sense of it being the last second. It was as though that second slowed down and He allowed me to feel the weightiness of it.

I was aware of its finality. There was no going back. I was aware of people who were headed for hell, but at the same time there was so much joy. I didn't understand how there could be such a duality in the weightiness of that last second coming to a close.

Then I was aware I was coming down through the atmosphere really fast. I could see the earth below and a gas station and a girl pumping gas. I knew I had to tell her she was in the last second and she had to hurry. "You have to know! You have to know now! The second is closing!" I was desperate to tell her she needed Jesus as savior before that last second closed.

At this point I was suddenly sitting up in bed and instinctively looking for pen and paper to write down what I knew I was about to hear. I started listening and writing. This is what I heard.

"Thus sayeth the Lord. Prophets rise up! Come forth! Come forth! The season is now. Winter is almost here. Spring forth now, for the snow fallest. The time has come to drink quickly. The dead are thirsty. Dawn is coming, it springs forth the light. The dust cometh together, yea they speaketh again. Get ready! Get ready! The hour is at hand. My hand is in the sky. The scenes are changing quickly. Come, come, come, don't be late! My invitation is closing. The ice crystal is forming in the sky. It's about to fall. The straw is shaking, can you not see it in your hand? It speaks. They're calling out Arise, Arise, Arise. Feel the cold air? The moisture is in the breath. Breathe! Breathe! Breathe! Saturate me now,

let me fill thy lungs with the living water. Joy is at hand, it's time to celebrate. Breathe in, hold out your hands. Let me fill them with living water. Look up in the night, face the heavens. The Gathering is soon. He is calling those who will listen. He has gathering those together outside, to watch the night sky. The canvas is in the left sky. When you see the scenes changing quickly, you will know it is time."

This third prophecy has many similarities to the one about the coming revival written down by Arthur Burt in 1930. Coming as it did on St Valentine's Day, it is significant as a picture of God's love in causing a chain of prophets to rise up to deliver the word of the Lord. As suggested by the Texas prophet, Bob's death marked the end of one era and signaled the new era of the Elijah Invitation.

In the face of a rising tide of militant Islam and the demonic deception perpetrated by AI and transhumanism, God is making a trumpet call to the Body of Christ. We are seeing a pattern in prophetic utterances and encounters; more believers are choosing to take up the invitation to the five-fold ministry; and a rising tide of believers is beginning to move in great power. When the Church is corporately positioned as a beach-head is when it will be empowered to usher in the Spirit of repentance and the last great world revival.

God is conducting a roll call. He is sending out the Elijah Invitation to His people. Will you be part of the corporate Elijah after the pattern of the Tishbite, or according to the pattern of John the Baptist? The question is: *which Elijah are you?*

Bibliography

Dick, Philip K., *Do Androids Dream of Electric Sheep?* Doubleday, 1968

———

Jorgensen, Owen, *Supernatural: The Life of William Branham.* Book Four: *The Evangelist and His Acclamation.* Tucson Tabernacle, 2555 North Stone Avenue, Tucson, Arizona 85705 USA, 2001

———

Kurzweil, Ray, *The Age of Intelligent Machines,* 1990

The Age of Spiritual Machines, 1999

The Singularity is Near: When Humans Transcend Biology, 2005

———

Shoebat, Walid, *God's War On Terror*, Top Executive Media, Newtown, 2008.

———

Unger, Craig, *House of Bush, House of Saud: The Hidden Relationship Between the World's Two Most Powerful Dynasties*, Scribner, 2004

———

Walsh, Toby, 2062: *The World That AI Made*, LaTrobe University Press, 2018

———

Warwick, Kevin, *I, Cyborg*, Century, London, 2002

Made in United States
Orlando, FL
02 July 2024

48552789R00093